Hidden Signs of the Universe

Decode the Secret Codes of Synchronicity, Signs, and Divine
Guidance to Understand the Real Meaning of Everything

Codex Occulto

ISBN: 979-8-89965-519-7
Imprint: Staten House

Staten House

Table of Contents

You're Not Going Crazy—You're Being Contacted

Have you ever experienced something so oddly timed, so improbably perfect or eerily repetitive, that it made you pause mid-step and wonder, What are the chances? Maybe you saw the same number over and over again on clocks, receipts, or license plates. Maybe a song came on the radio with lyrics that seemed to speak directly to your situation. Or perhaps, during a moment of intense inner turmoil, a butterfly landed quietly on your shoulder, staying just long enough to shift your mood. These moments are more than poetic anomalies. They are signals. Subtle nudges. Quiet communications from a larger intelligence.

This book is about those signs—the hidden language of the Universe that whispers, guides, and sometimes even shouts to get your attention. And no, you're not crazy for noticing. You're not imagining things or reading too much into coincidence. In fact, the very fact that you're noticing them may mean you're finally becoming aware of a deeper dialogue happening all around you.

Most people don't listen because they haven't been taught how to. We live in a world dominated by noise—alerts, agendas, and logic-based reasoning. We're trained to trust only what we can quantify, explain, or reproduce in a lab. But reality isn't built solely from data; it's built from energy, resonance, and meaning. And sometimes meaning shows up in mysterious ways.

This book isn't about dogma or religious belief. It's not about telling you what to think. Instead, it's about tuning your inner instruments so you can better hear what's already being said—to you, for you. We'll dive into how signs work, why they matter, and how to tell the difference between a true message and wishful thinking. You'll learn to interpret the Universe's clues not as random, but as precise tools meant to help you live with more clarity, connection, and courage.

The truth is, life isn't meant to be a guessing game. The Universe—God, Source, the Field, whatever name fits your framework—wants you to know. The signs are everywhere. You just have to know how to see.

By the end of this journey, you'll have more than stories of synchronicities. You'll have a toolkit for recognizing, decoding, and living in alignment with the greater intelligence that surrounds and flows through everything. It's time to stop asking if the signs are real, and start asking what they're trying to say.

PART I: OPENING THE CHANNEL

Chapter 1: Why the Universe Speaks in Signs

The Universe does not speak English, French, or Mandarin. It speaks in a language far more universal: **symbols, frequencies, patterns, and resonance.** This symbolic language isn't linear like our spoken sentences. It's layered, often metaphorical, and designed to bypass the analytical mind to speak directly to the soul.

Think about dreams—how often do they defy logic but still carry meaning? A dream of flying isn't about gravity; it's about freedom, perspective, or release. In the same way, a recurring number pattern might not carry arithmetic significance, but emotional or energetic weight. This is how the Universe speaks: indirectly, poetically, and personally.

Why would a vast, intelligent field of consciousness communicate this way? Because symbols allow multiple layers of truth to co-exist. They adapt to each person's inner world, allowing a sign to mean one thing to you and something slightly different to another—both correct. Language can be manipulated, doubted, or misinterpreted. Symbols, especially when felt intuitively, cut deeper. They're not just seen; they're recognized.

Energetic Laws and Divine Timing

In the fabric of existence, everything is energy—vibrating, resonating, attracting or repelling. The **Law of Vibration**, one of the foundational energetic laws, posits that everything—thoughts, emotions, objects—vibrates at a particular frequency. When your internal state shifts, so does your external reality. And the Universe reflects those shifts back to you through signs.

This is why you'll often notice more synchronicities or meaningful "coincidences" when you're going through a period of transformation. Your vibration is changing, and the Universe responds. Signs begin to appear not as random events, but as a kind of **feedback loop**, mirroring your inner evolution.

Closely related is the concept of **divine timing**—the idea that everything unfolds not on our schedule, but in accordance with a larger rhythm. Signs often arrive not when we want them, but when we're ready to receive them. That readiness isn't always conscious. Sometimes, your soul knows you're ready long before your mind does.

So if a particular symbol or message keeps appearing in your life, it's worth asking: What am I energetically aligned with right now? What is life trying to show me—not later, but now?

The Role of Free Will

One of the most fascinating aspects of the Universe's communication system is that it doesn't force itself on you. It whispers, nudges, repeats—but never overrides your will. That's because **free will is sacred.** You're allowed to ignore the signs, dismiss them, or explain them away. You can choose not to act, not to trust, not to see.

But here's the paradox: the more you choose to notice, the more the Universe speaks. It's a relationship, not a one-way broadcast. When you begin to acknowledge the signs, interpret them, and respond, you're essentially saying, I'm listening. And like any good dialogue partner, the Universe opens up when it knows it's being heard.

This also explains why some people seem to receive more signs than others—it's not favoritism, it's **receptivity.** The signs may be everywhere, but only the tuned-in are aware of them. That awareness is something you can cultivate.

You don't need to become psychic or radically mystical. You simply need to become curious. Pay attention. And most importantly, be willing to suspend disbelief long enough to ask: What if this means something?

Because more often than not, it does.

Chapter 2: The Art of Noticing: Rewiring for Awareness

We are constantly surrounded by messages, patterns, and signals. But most of us are too distracted to notice them. The issue isn't the absence of signs—it's our inability to see them. In a world of overstimulation and multitasking, our attention is splintered. The art of noticing is not about having supernatural gifts; it's about slowing down, refining perception, and retraining the brain to pick up on subtle cues that were always there.

Reconnecting with the Universe's symbolic language requires a shift in your mental operating system. You must learn to listen differently, see through a new lens, and give value to things that once seemed mundane or coincidental. This is not magic—it's mindfulness sharpened to a fine edge. In this Chapter, we'll explore how to tune your awareness, how your brain actually filters reality, and how you can reprogram yourself to see what most overlook.

Rewriting the Filters of Perception

From birth, your brain is trained to filter reality. Every second, your senses take in an overwhelming amount of data—far more than you can consciously process. So your brain develops shortcuts: it highlights what it considers important and ignores the rest. This is helpful for basic survival, but terrible for spiritual receptivity.

Most of your perception is **pattern-based and expectation-driven.** What you see is not a neutral reflection of reality; it's a reflection of what you've been taught to look for. If you don't expect magic, you won't see it. If you believe the world is random, your brain will reinforce randomness. But if you start to believe that life is alive with meaning, your filters begin to adjust. Suddenly, you notice more. You feel more. You see more.

This is called **reticular activation**—a function of the brain's Reticular Activating System (RAS), which acts like a selective spotlight. Ever notice that when you're thinking about buying a red car, you suddenly start seeing red cars everywhere? That's the RAS at work. The same principle applies to signs from the Universe. Once you train your RAS to flag synchronicities, number patterns, or symbolic events, they'll begin to pop into awareness more frequently. They were always there; now you're tuned in.

Rewriting your filters doesn't mean turning into a paranoid decoder of every minor event. It means consciously choosing to open your senses and reassign importance to things that used to slip past you. It's a skill—and it's one you can train.

Slowing Down to Speed Up Awareness

One of the most radical acts you can take in a distracted world is to slow down.

Awareness doesn't rise from the frantic pace of to-do lists and screen time; it blossoms in stillness, presence, and curiosity. The signs that matter most are rarely loud. They're quiet, almost humble, and easy to miss if you're always rushing.

Slowing down doesn't mean dropping your responsibilities or moving through life at a snail's pace. It means creating **moments of intentional pause.** It's the few extra seconds you spend observing your environment. The breath you take before responding to something reactive. The way you start to really look at people, trees, billboards, the lyrics of a passing song—not as background noise, but as potential messengers.

You begin to treat your surroundings as a dialogue instead of a dead set. Reality becomes more responsive. This isn't just poetic thinking; it's rooted in neuroscience and quantum principles that suggest the observer affects the observed. When you pay closer attention, reality shifts to meet your gaze.

Daily rituals can help support this slowness: morning journaling, a walk without headphones, simply sitting in silence with a question in mind. These aren't just wellness habits—they're invitations to enter into a co-creative relationship with the world. In slowness, you create space for signs to show up. You start to live in a more spacious version of time—kairos time, not chronos time. Not clock time, but divine timing.

And as your perception of time loosens, so does your grip on control. You become more open to surprise, to guidance, to receiving. Your intuition sharpens. You stop bulldozing through life and start listening for the next cue.

Cultivating a Curiosity Mindset

At the heart of noticing is one vital quality: **curiosity.** Children notice everything because they haven't been trained to tune things out. They ask endless questions, investigate the smallest anomalies, and treat the world as something worth discovering. To live a life rich in signs, you must reclaim this childlike mindset.

Curiosity doesn't mean forcing meaning onto everything—it means staying open to meaning. It's the difference between skepticism and inquiry. Skepticism says, "This can't be real." Inquiry says, "What if it is?" That openness creates a mental environment in which synchronicities can flourish.

Start by asking small, sacred questions as you move through your day:

- What wants to be seen right now?

- Is there something I've been ignoring that keeps showing up?

- If this moment were trying to tell me something, what might it be?

These are not questions to analyze to death. They're prompts to help soften your attention and invite more fluid perception. Curiosity is not about fixing; it's about exploring. When something strange happens—say, three people mention the same book to you in a week—ask yourself, What thread is the Universe inviting me to follow?

Curiosity keeps your energy playful and receptive. And signs are more likely to show up when you're in that state. If you become rigid or overly logical, you close the aperture. But if you treat the world like an interactive storybook—one where symbols can leap off the page and speak directly to you—everything becomes alive with possibility.

The more you practice this mindset, the more natural it becomes. Eventually, it won't feel like practice at all. You'll simply live in a world that communicates constantly, and your job will be to listen, follow, and trust.

Paying Attention

Noticing signs isn't about spiritual elitism. It's not reserved for gurus, psychics, or mystics. It's a basic human ability that's atrophied from underuse—but can be reignited with attention, presence, and a curious heart. When you slow down, rewrite your perceptual filters, and begin to see reality not as static but as interactive, a new dimension opens up.

The art of noticing is the first essential step toward living a guided life. Before interpretation, before action, comes simple awareness. And from that awareness, a new relationship with the Universe is born—one where you don't just move through life, but participate in it as a conversation.

Are you paying attention? Good. Because the Universe already is.

Chapter 3: The Signal vs. The Noise

As your awareness sharpens and you begin to notice more signs in your life, a new challenge arises: not every strange coincidence or emotional nudge is a message from the Universe. In a world overflowing with stimuli, how do you tell the difference between a real signal and meaningless noise? This is where discernment becomes essential.

The modern mind is flooded with distractions—push notifications, breaking news, social media reels, and a thousand internal thoughts competing for your focus. In this chaos, it's easy to mistake anxiety for intuition, a random event for a divine message, or background clutter for a spiritual sign. To live in true alignment, you need to become a discerning receiver—able to recognize not just the volume of signs, but their clarity, resonance, and truth.

This Chapter is about separating what matters from what doesn't. You'll learn how to filter through the clutter of modern life, listen for authentic signals, and trust your own body and energy field as a compass for truth.

How the Modern World Muffles Your Inner Frequency

Our ancestors lived in a world where messages from nature, the body, and dreams were taken seriously. They paid attention to the direction of the wind, the appearance of certain animals, the feeling in their gut. In today's world, that inner radar has been largely replaced by algorithms, advertising, and constant connectivity. As a result, our intuitive muscles have atrophied. We've outsourced our inner knowing to screens, schedules, and other people's opinions.

The average person is exposed to over 10,000 marketing messages per day. That's not counting news headlines, emails, personal dramas, and inner self-talk. Most of this information is irrelevant, fear-based, or agenda-driven. It doesn't nourish your soul or elevate your awareness—it drowns it.

To hear the Universe clearly, you have to reduce the noise. That doesn't mean becoming a hermit or deleting every app. It means becoming conscious of what you're consuming and how it affects your nervous system. Information is energy. And not all energy is neutral.

Ask yourself regularly:

- Is this input calming or agitating me?
- Is it expanding my awareness or narrowing it?
- Does this help me connect with myself or disconnect from myself?

When you become more selective with your attention, you begin to make space for genuine signals to rise to the surface. You notice the timing of events more clearly. You feel the difference between your anxiety and your intuition. You start to hear something deeper: your own soul's signal, finally cutting through the static.

Your Inner Tuning Fork: Recognizing Resonance

Not all signs feel the same. Some hit you like a jolt of electricity. Others arrive quietly, like a whisper only you can hear. One of the most important ways to distinguish signal from noise is by learning to recognize **resonance.** Resonance is that unmistakable inner click, that "yes" feeling you get—not in your brain, but in your body and heart.

This is where the intellect must take a back seat. The mind is excellent at rationalizing, comparing, and doubting. But resonance bypasses logic. It's a felt sense. A symbol, message, or event might not make analytical sense, but you'll know it matters because it lands. It stirs something in you. It pulls your attention with a magnetism you can't explain.

This is your inner tuning fork. And like any instrument, it becomes more accurate the more you use it.

Try this simple practice: when something odd or repetitive happens—a number pattern, a line from a song, a recurring image—pause and check in with your body. Do you feel a quickening in your chest? Goosebumps? A sense of peace or curiosity? These are signs of energetic resonance. If, on the other hand, the event leaves you confused, numb, or tense, it may be noise—or it may simply not be meant for you at this time.

Also, note the **emotional echo** of a moment. Sometimes the impact of a sign doesn't register immediately. But hours later, you're still thinking about it. That lingering awareness is another clue that something deeper is at play. Real signals leave an imprint. They carry a frequency that stays with you, even after the moment passes.

The more you tune into this felt sense, the more confident you become in separating what's meaningful from what's just mental clutter. You begin to trust your inner response more than external explanations.

Patterns, Persistence, and the Universe's Delivery System

One-off events can be interesting, but real signs often arrive in **patterns.** The Universe tends to repeat itself when it wants your attention. If you miss the signal the first time, it doesn't get angry—it gets louder, or more creative. This persistence is one of the clearest ways to tell you're being contacted.

If you've seen the same number sequence three times today, or the same animal shows up in wildly different settings, or people keep mentioning a book, place, or person out of nowhere—that's not randomness. That's delivery confirmation. The Universe will use multiple channels—sight, sound, people, dreams—to send the same message until you notice.

Pay attention to the **clusters**. One butterfly might be a coincidence. Three butterflies in unrelated situations on a day when you're contemplating a major life decision? That's more than metaphor. That's symbolic intervention.

Another helpful guideline: **specificity over vagueness.** Signs that hit home tend to be precise. They arrive at moments of internal questioning or emotional intensity. They feel timed, not arbitrary. And they often "answer" a question you didn't say out loud but were quietly carrying in your heart.

Still, be cautious of reading too much into every pattern. Some repetition is natural. The difference between a real sign and noise dressed up as meaning is that real signs feel **timely, targeted, and alive**. They engage you at multiple levels—mental, emotional, and energetic.

That's why tracking helps. Keep a journal of symbols, patterns, and events that seem significant. You'll begin to see the threads. Some won't make sense until later, but hindsight often reveals the orchestration behind what once felt random.

You're not making these things happen—you're simply starting to notice the elegant choreography of a Universe that's always communicating in layers.

Active Listening

Learning to distinguish signal from noise is a crucial milestone in your spiritual growth. It marks the shift from passive noticing to **active listening.** It's the difference between being curious and being wise. Signs are real, but so is projection. And in a world designed to hijack your attention, your clarity is your superpower.

By reducing distractions, tuning into your body's resonance, and watching for persistent, patterned signals, you become a clear receiver. The messages will come through more often, and with greater clarity. You'll waste less time second-guessing. You'll start to trust the moments that land, and release the ones that don't.

The Universe is always speaking. But to hear it well, you must learn to filter out the static. When you do, you discover something profound: the guidance you've been seeking is not only around you—it's already in you, waiting to be heard.

Chapter 4: When You Ask, It Answers

One of the most startling discoveries you can make on a spiritual path is this: the Universe is not silent. It responds. Not just occasionally, not just to the chosen few, but consistently and intimately—especially when you begin to ask the right kinds of questions. Most people don't receive signs not because they're unworthy or unconnected, but because they've never asked. Or they've asked without the belief that an answer would actually come.

Asking is not about begging or demanding. It's about aligning your intention with curiosity and trust. It's an energetic request, not just a mental one. And the moment you ask with presence and sincerity, you create a ripple. That ripple doesn't vanish—it activates something. A response begins forming, though not always in the way or timing you expect.

This Chapter is about that sacred exchange—the moment where desire meets dialogue, where questions meet clues, and where your willingness to ask opens the door for guidance to find you.

The Power of Clear Intention

Before a sign can find you, you must initiate the relationship. That doesn't mean you have to meditate for hours or chant under a full moon. It simply means you have to be **clear in your desire to communicate.** Intention is everything in the language of signs. It's the tuning fork that calls forth a matching vibration from the field of reality.

When your mind is scattered, your energy is, too. But when you focus—even briefly—on a specific question or area of your life where you're seeking guidance, you send out a pulse. That pulse is not just emotional or mental. It's **energetic**. And energy moves faster than words. It crosses boundaries the logical mind can't.

Try this: instead of just thinking, "I need help," form a more precise inner question, like:

- "What would bring me more peace in this situation?"
- "Show me what I'm not seeing clearly."
- "Am I moving in the right direction with this decision?"

Notice that these are not questions of control. They are questions of insight, alignment, and clarity. When you ask in this way, you are not begging for an outcome—you are inviting communication. You are stepping into co-creation, not manipulation.

This is important: **intention does not guarantee a specific result.** It opens a channel for guidance. The Universe may answer with affirmation, redirection, or even silence—but that silence, too, can be meaningful. Sometimes it means: Not yet. Or: You already know. Asking with openness rather than expectation is how you stay in flow.

Why the Answer Doesn't Always Look Like One

One of the most misunderstood aspects of spiritual communication is that answers from the Universe rarely come in the way we imagine. You may ask for a sign, then expect a glowing billboard or a lightning bolt. More often, what you'll get is something far subtler: a conversation that suddenly shifts your perspective, a book that falls off the shelf, a dream that lingers, a strange detour that leads you exactly where you need to be.

The key is not to demand that the Universe speak in your language. It speaks in **its own dialect**—a fusion of metaphor, energy, and timing. Your job is not to control the delivery system, but to develop the capacity to recognize the reply.

Imagine sending out a radio broadcast. You don't control who calls in, but when someone does, you learn to listen carefully. Some answers will feel loud and instant. Others will arrive days or weeks later, weaving themselves into the background until the pattern becomes obvious. And sometimes, the message doesn't come through the sky or a screen—it comes from you. A sudden realization. A shift in emotion. A knowing that wasn't there before.

This is why journaling your questions helps. It marks the moment you asked. Later, you can trace how the answer unfolded—through symbols, through people, through changes in feeling. You begin to see the cause-and-effect chain between your intention and reality's response.

It's also why the practice of **letting go** is essential. Ask your question. Feel it. Then release it. Obsessing over the answer constricts the space in which it can arrive. When you plant a seed, you don't dig it up every hour to see if it's growing. You water it. You give it light. And then you trust.

The Feedback Loop of Asking and Receiving

When you ask and receive—even once—you activate what could be called a **feedback loop of trust.** That one moment of guidance, when it clicks, builds confidence. You begin to believe. That belief sharpens your awareness. Sharper awareness leads to more signs. And the cycle continues.

Many people ask but don't notice the answer because they've already decided how it should look. But once you let the Universe answer on its own terms, you're often stunned by the accuracy and personal nature of the response. It will use your language, your history, your humor. The signs will feel tailored. Because they are.

And the more you notice, the more the Universe seems to respond. This doesn't mean you become dependent on signs for every step. It means you learn to walk in partnership with something greater—like consulting a wise mentor before a major move. Eventually, that inner guidance becomes part of you. You don't always need to ask; you simply know.

Still, asking is powerful—not because the Universe wouldn't guide you otherwise, but because asking makes you available. It shifts your vibration from passive to engaged. It reminds you that you are not at the mercy of life, but in relationship with it.

Here's something else to remember: **you can ask for confirmation.** If you receive a sign and aren't sure whether it was real, ask again. Say, "If this was a true message, show me another sign I can clearly recognize." If the signs are real, they will build upon each other. The Universe doesn't tire of you. It only asks that you pay attention.

And if the signs stop coming? Don't panic. Often, that's a sign in itself. You may be in a phase of integration, not instruction. Silence can be sacred, too. A pause between breaths. A clearing before the next message.

Asking, receiving, trusting—this is the cycle of spiritual dialogue. It is not one-way. It is not rare. It is not elite. It is accessible, living, and waiting to be used.

Asking is the secret

When you ask, it answers. Not always in the way you imagined, but always in a way that's aligned with your path. The moment you step into curiosity with intention, you awaken an ancient relationship—a line of communication between your soul and the vast, intelligent fabric of reality.

Asking is not weakness. It's wisdom. It's the awareness that you are not alone, not abandoned, not spinning in a cold, indifferent universe. You are surrounded by intelligence, synchronicity, and guidance. And that guidance responds to engagement.

Start asking—not just when you're desperate, but when you're ready to listen. Ask not only for direction, but for alignment. Not only for clarity, but for peace. The Universe hears all of it.

And somewhere, a sign is already on its way.

PART II: THE TYPES OF SIGNS

Chapter 5: Synchronicities: The Cosmic Wink

Few experiences feel more enchanting—or more perplexing—than synchronicity. You think of a friend you haven't heard from in years, and they text you that afternoon. You're pondering a career shift when a stranger in the checkout line starts talking about your exact dilemma. Or you open a book at random and find a passage that answers the question you didn't even know how to ask.

At first glance, these may seem like coincidences. But they often carry a different weight—one that feels designed, orchestrated, or at the very least, charged with unusual timing. That's because they are. Synchronicity is one of the most recognizable ways the Universe signals its presence in your life. It's not a random occurrence—it's a cosmic wink, a way of saying, Yes, I see you. Keep going.

This Chapter explores what synchronicity really is, how it differs from simple chance, and how to recognize the deeper guidance it offers. As we'll see, synchronicities are more than charming episodes—they're evidence of the interconnected field that links thought, energy, and meaning in perfect, elegant ways.

What Is Synchronicity, Really?

The term synchronicity was coined by Swiss psychologist Carl Jung, who defined it as the "meaningful coincidence of two or more events where something other than probability of chance is involved." In other words, a synchronicity occurs when two events align in a way that is both improbable and deeply meaningful to the observer, even though there appears to be no direct causal link.

What makes synchronicities special is not just their timing, but their **personal resonance**. They often reflect something you're actively processing internally. The coincidence alone isn't the message—the meaning you assign to it is what turns it into a sign.

Jung believed synchronicities reflected a connection between the inner world (psyche) and the outer world (matter)—a unifying field where mind and reality are not separate but co-creative. In modern language, we might say that synchronicity happens when your inner frequency "pings" the universe and the universe "pings" you back through an external event.

Importantly, synchronicity is not something you force. You don't go hunting for them, and you can't manufacture their timing. They appear most often when you're in alignment, in transition, or in need of encouragement. They're not interruptions to life; they are life communicating with you at a deeper level.

The Emotional Impact of a Synchronicity

While science may struggle to quantify synchronicity, your nervous system knows exactly when it's happening. There's often a visceral reaction—a feeling of amazement, warmth, or emotional clarity. Your body may tingle, your heart may beat faster, or a tear might well up. That's not sentimentality—it's recognition. It's the soul saying, I've been seen.

This emotional impact is one of the surest ways to distinguish a true synchronicity from mere coincidence. Coincidences can be curious. Synchronicities hit you in the chest. They often land during moments of inner questioning or uncertainty, serving as confirmation, affirmation, or even redirection.

For example, you might be unsure whether to move to a new city. While walking down the street, you overhear someone talking about that exact city, then open your inbox to see a job posting there. You feel a surge of energy—not just curiosity, but a pull. That's the emotional marker of synchronicity. The outer world reflects the inner terrain, and it touches you deeply because it feels tailored to your experience.

That emotional resonance is not to be dismissed. The Universe does not just speak in symbols—it speaks through feeling. Synchronicities are one way it delivers messages directly to your emotional body, bypassing overthinking and reaching into something older, deeper, and wiser within you.

Recognizing the Web of Meaning

To truly understand synchronicity, you must accept a radical premise: the Universe is not random. It is intelligent, interconnected, and responsive. Every thought, intention, and emotion you emit becomes part of the web—a signal that can trigger other responses, events, and alignments in the physical world.

This doesn't mean you control everything. But it does mean that your **state of being** shapes what you notice, attract, and intersect with. Synchronicities are often the result of **energetic coherence**—when your inner world is in resonance with a particular frequency, the external world responds in kind.

If you're deeply focused on healing, for instance, you may begin to encounter books, people, or phrases that speak directly to your healing journey. This isn't just good luck. It's the web of meaning at work. And the more conscious you are of your internal state, the more likely you are to spot these connections.

Interestingly, synchronicities often arrive during **threshold moments**—times of transition, decision-making, or inner awakening. That's because these moments create openings in your field. You're more alert, more sensitive, and more willing to consider guidance beyond logic. The Universe meets that openness with mirrors.

It's also worth noting that synchronicity thrives on **attention.** The more you acknowledge it, the more frequently it tends to occur. This is not superstition—it's neuroplasticity. As you validate synchronicities, you reinforce the neural pathways that allow you to perceive more of them. It becomes easier to see the pattern in what once looked like noise.

A practical tool for deepening this relationship is to **track your synchronicities**. Keep a journal or note on your phone where you document them as they arise. Record the timing, the details, and how they made you feel. Over time, you'll begin to see larger patterns—a constellation of signs that form a map. And you'll realize something stunning: you are never alone in this journey.

Not Accidents

Synchronicities are not accidents. They are exquisitely timed affirmations that the invisible forces guiding your life are very real—and very aware of you. Whether they show up as repeated names, uncanny timings, or whispered truths from a stranger, their purpose is the same: to let you know that your inner and outer worlds are not separate, but dancing together in sacred rhythm.

They remind you that you are not wandering in the dark. You are walking in step with something greater. And every so often, the Universe leans in and winks.

You're exactly where you need to be.

Chapter 6: Numbers, Repeats, and Sacred Math

You glance at the clock: 11:11. Later, your receipt total is $33.33. A license plate with 777 catches your eye, and then your hotel room is 444. These repeating numbers seem to follow you, popping up at uncanny moments—especially during times of emotional intensity, decision-making, or transformation. At first, you might brush it off as coincidence. But the repetition becomes hard to ignore. And at some point, you begin to ask: What does this mean?

Numbers are one of the most common ways the Universe speaks. Unlike language, which changes across cultures and eras, numbers are universal. Their shapes, patterns, and sequences carry vibrational meanings that transcend words. This Chapter explores how numbers function as signals from the greater field of intelligence, why certain sequences recur in your life, and how to begin interpreting them through both intuition and pattern.

When you start paying attention to repeating numbers, you're not being superstitious. You're tapping into one of the oldest symbolic systems on Earth: sacred math.

Why the Universe Uses Numbers

Numbers are the DNA of reality. From the spirals of galaxies to the symmetry of leaves, from planetary orbits to the timing of your breath, the entire physical world follows mathematical patterns. The ancient Greek philosopher Pythagoras believed that numbers were not just quantities but qualities—living archetypes with energetic meaning. In his system, 1 represented unity, 2 duality, 3 harmony, and so on. These ideas aren't just historical curiosities—they're echoed in modern quantum theory, where reality is seen as vibrating energy, structured by mathematical law.

So when the Universe sends you a repeating number—say, 111 or 555—it's not just sending a signal. It's aligning you with a **vibration.** The number becomes a shorthand for a larger message or state of being. And because numbers can appear in countless neutral contexts—clocks, prices, addresses—they make ideal vehicles for synchronicity. They don't require mystical scenery or rare timing. They're hidden in plain sight, which makes them perfect tools for the subtle communications of the Universe.

Numbers also bypass language and cultural filters. You don't have to speak a certain language to understand the feeling of seeing 333 repeatedly. The recognition is energetic first, cognitive second. You feel the pattern before you try to analyze it. That's by design.

And once you begin noticing repeating numbers, they often become **personalized.** You may find, for example, that 444 always shows up when you're in alignment, or that 222 appears when you're avoiding a truth. Over time, a language emerges between you and the Universe—one built from digits, repetition, and resonance.

Understanding Repeating Number Sequences

Repeating numbers, sometimes called "angel numbers," are the most common numeric signs people report. While different schools of thought offer different interpretations, there are some widely accepted meanings associated with these sequences. Let's explore a few of the most frequently seen ones—not as dogma, but as starting points for personal reflection.

111 – Alignment and Awakening

This number often shows up at the beginning of a new cycle or spiritual awakening. It signals that your thoughts are manifesting quickly, and that your internal state is closely reflected in your external reality. It's a reminder to stay conscious of your focus and to choose intentions wisely.

222 – Balance and Relationships

When 222 appears, it often relates to harmony, partnership, or duality. It can signal a time to seek balance in your life, or confirmation that relationships (romantic or otherwise) are developing in divine timing. It also suggests patience—things are aligning even if you can't yet see it.

333 – Guidance and Expansion

This sequence is commonly interpreted as a sign that you are supported by higher energies—guides, ancestors, or the Universe itself. It's often seen when you are being nudged to step into a larger version of yourself, especially in creative or spiritual pursuits.

444 – Foundation and Protection

Seeing 444 may suggest that you are building something important—a career, relationship, or inner structure—and that you are protected in the process. It's a reminder to stay grounded and trust your process, even if the road ahead feels uncertain.

555 – Change and Transition

This number almost always shows up around major changes. It's a clear sign that transformation is underway, whether by choice or necessity. It encourages you to release what no longer fits and trust that what's coming is more aligned.

666 – Recalibration and Self-Reflection

Often misunderstood due to religious fear, 666 is not inherently negative. It usually signals that your focus is overly external or material, and you're being called back to balance. It's an invitation to reflect, reset, and realign with what matters most.

777 – Divine Insight and Miracles

When 777 appears, it's often a confirmation that you're in a high-frequency state. It suggests spiritual clarity, intuitive flow, and even small miracles unfolding behind the scenes. It's a cosmic pat on the back—keep going.

888 – Abundance and Completion

This number signals financial or energetic abundance and often appears when a cycle is completing successfully. It can also mean that karma is being resolved, or that a long effort is about to bear fruit.

999 – Endings and Evolution

Seeing 999 is a sign that something is coming to a close. It's not just an end—it's a graduation. This number often signals that you're being prepared for a new Chapter, and that it's time to release the old to make space for what's next.

While these interpretations offer useful entry points, it's crucial to remember that **your relationship with numbers is personal.** Your emotional response matters more than any list of meanings. If a certain number gives you peace, power, or clarity, that is its meaning for you. Trust your internal dictionary.

When Patterns Become Personal Portals

At first, you might see repeating numbers occasionally—maybe once a week or during moments of stress. But the more you acknowledge them, the more they appear. Eventually, they stop feeling random and start feeling **orchestrated.** That's not imagination—it's engagement. You're co-creating a language.

Over time, you may begin to develop a private lexicon of numbers. Maybe 144 always shows up when you're doubting yourself, or 717 appears when you're on the verge of a breakthrough. You'll notice which ones come as warnings, which ones come as encouragement. Numbers become markers—like breadcrumbs on a spiritual trail, guiding you toward alignment.

You may also find that your birthdate, house number, or even phone number carries repeating digits that take on new meaning over time. These become anchors—numerical totems that ground your attention and remind you of your path.

It's worth keeping a number journal to record these sightings and your impressions. Over time, patterns will emerge—not just in the numbers, but in the context: what you were thinking, how you were feeling, what decision you were wrestling with. That's where the real value lies. Numbers don't just appear to get your attention. They appear to **mirror your energy.** They confirm that something meaningful is unfolding, even if you can't see it yet.

Eventually, these moments no longer feel supernatural—they feel natural. You come to expect a responsive Universe. You trust that meaning isn't something you have to chase; it's something you allow, observe, and honor.

Universe and Numbers

Repeating numbers are more than curious alignments. They are living signals from the energetic matrix that underlies reality—vibrational nudges designed to help you stay conscious, aligned, and awake. They don't dictate your path, but they do illuminate it. They show you when you're in flow, when you're being called to shift, and when unseen support is present.

You don't need to understand sacred geometry or numerology to be moved by 11:11 appearing on your clock during a moment of doubt. You only need to be willing to ask, What is this moment trying to tell me?

Numbers are everywhere. But when you begin to notice their repetition, rhythm, and resonance, you stop seeing them as background noise—and start receiving them as messengers.

The Universe is counting with you. Every digit is a whisper. Every sequence, a sign.

Chapter 7: Dreams and Symbolic Downloads

Each night, when the conscious mind loosens its grip and the ego dissolves into sleep, another world opens. It is vast, surreal, and layered with symbols that don't follow the rules of logic but speak directly to your inner being. This is the realm of dreams—and it is one of the most potent spaces for receiving signs from the Universe.

Far from being random or meaningless, dreams offer symbolic downloads from your subconscious and beyond. They're more than mental echoes of the day; they are bridges—connecting your waking life with deeper truths, unresolved emotions, and sometimes even spiritual guidance. The dream world strips away the filters of the rational mind and allows the soul to speak in its native language: metaphor.

This Chapter explores how to understand the symbolic nature of dreams, why they carry intuitive messages, and how to work with them as a tool for guidance and awakening. Once you begin to honor dreams as more than psychological leftovers, you'll discover a powerful inner universe that is constantly revealing what you need to see, feel, or do next.

The Dream Realm as a Portal to the Inner Self

Dreams are more than neurological processes. They are psychic terrain—territory where the deepest parts of your being play out emotions, fears, desires, and spiritual questions through rich symbolic landscapes. While science often reduces dreams to mere brain activity, ancient wisdom traditions have always viewed dreaming as a sacred function. Indigenous cultures, mystics, and seers from around the world have long considered dreams to be prophetic, revelatory, and deeply meaningful.

From this perspective, dreams are a **conversation** between your higher self and your waking self. They emerge not from the noise of the mind, but from the quiet intelligence that lies beneath. The problem isn't that dreams are vague; it's that we've forgotten how to read them.

You might dream of being chased, flying, drowning, walking through endless doors, or speaking with someone who's passed away. These images are not literal—they're symbolic. A flood might represent emotional overwhelm. A house might symbolize the state of your psyche. Being lost might reflect a lack of direction in your waking life. The key is not to interpret these images using rigid, one-size-fits-all dictionaries, but to ask: What does this image mean to me? What part of me is trying to be seen or healed?

Dreams bypass ego defenses and speak in emotional truth. They'll show you the fears you won't admit, the desires you've buried, and the possibilities your waking mind can't yet grasp. And sometimes, they'll deliver guidance so precise it feels otherworldly—because it is.

You don't have to be a trained analyst to benefit from your dreams. You simply have to pay attention and be willing to engage with them not as riddles, but as reflections of your soul's deeper journey.

Types of Symbolic and Prophetic Dreams

Not all dreams are created equal. Some are fragmented replays of your day—mental housekeeping. But others carry a different weight. These are the ones you remember vividly, the ones that stay with you for hours or days. These are **symbolic dreams**, and sometimes even **prophetic dreams**—dreams that reveal insight about your life, direction, or future events with startling clarity.

Here are some common types of meaningful dreams and what they might be offering:

1. The Recurring Dream

If a dream shows up again and again, especially over months or years, it's not just your brain glitching. It's your soul insisting on being heard. Recurring dreams are often tied to unresolved emotional material or repeating patterns in your waking life. The repetition is not random—it's a sign that something requires your conscious attention.

2. The Lucid Dream

In a lucid dream, you become aware that you're dreaming while still inside the dream. This level of awareness can open up powerful possibilities for healing and self-discovery. In some cases, lucid dreaming allows you to ask direct questions to dream characters or explore symbolic spaces with intention. Many report receiving clear messages or even spiritual guidance during these states.

3. The Visitation Dream

Sometimes, those who have passed on appear in our dreams—not as figments of memory, but as fully present beings who communicate with us directly. These dreams are often marked by a deep sense of peace or clarity. They may bring closure, comfort, or even warnings. While skeptics may call them hallucinations, many who experience them feel that something real—beyond the personal subconscious—was at play.

4. The Prophetic or Insight Dream

These dreams don't always predict the future in dramatic detail, but they often reveal truths you haven't yet recognized in waking life. They might show the outcome of a relationship, the energy of a decision, or the presence of something you've been avoiding. Sometimes, people report dreaming about events before they happen—meeting someone they later encounter, seeing a place they've never been, or sensing changes before they unfold. These dreams suggest that the subconscious—or even the soul—can access information not yet known to the rational mind.

5. The Symbolic Drama

Most dreams fall into this category—a symbolic narrative that reflects something emotionally charged within you. You might be falling, trapped, soaring, running, or navigating strange landscapes. These dreams are rich in metaphor and are deeply personal. Their power lies not in being "decoded" by someone else, but in how they make you feel and what they mirror about your current internal state.

By paying attention to these types of dreams—and especially the ones that stir emotion—you begin to receive the symbolic downloads your higher self has been trying to deliver all along.

How to Work with Dreams as Guidance

To access the wisdom of your dreams, you must first start remembering them. That means building a relationship with your dream life and signaling to your subconscious that you're ready to listen.

1. Set an Intention Before Sleep

Before going to bed, take a moment to ask for guidance or clarity. You might say something simple like, "I am open to receiving meaningful dreams tonight. Please help me remember them." The act of asking sets the stage for deeper dreaming and strengthens the bridge between your conscious and subconscious mind.

2. Keep a Dream Journal

Place a notebook by your bed and write down your dreams immediately upon waking—even if they seem nonsensical or fragmented. Over time, themes and symbols will emerge. Patterns will reveal themselves. And the mere act of recording your dreams will strengthen your recall and deepen your engagement.

3. Reflect, Don't Analyze

Approach your dreams with curiosity rather than a need for exact answers. ask yourself:

- How did I feel in this dream?

- What symbols stood out most?

- What part of my waking life does this mirror?

34

- If this dream were offering advice, what would it be?

This reflective approach allows insight to rise naturally, rather than forcing meaning onto the symbols. Often, the emotional tone of the dream reveals more than the imagery itself.

4. Look for Echoes in Waking Life

Many signs first appear in dreams and then echo into your waking life. A symbol from your dream might show up in a conversation, a movie scene, or a chance encounter the next day. These "echoes" validate the dream's importance and invite you to keep listening.

Over time, you'll develop your own symbolic dictionary—one not found in books but written through lived experience. That dictionary becomes one of your most intimate tools for spiritual navigation.

The Reality of Dreams

Dreams are not distractions from real life—they are part of real life. They are not confined to sleep—they influence the waking world, shaping how we understand ourselves and what we are becoming. When you learn to honor your dreams, you gain access to a powerful stream of inner guidance, emotional processing, and cosmic communication.

The Universe often speaks most clearly when your guard is down, your mind is quiet, and your soul is open. That's the gift of dreaming. It's not just rest. It's revelation.

And every night, the signs return—waiting for you to notice, receive, and remember.

Chapter 8: Animals, Objects, and Repeating Patterns

Not all signs are abstract or internal. Sometimes, the Universe chooses the physical world as its chalkboard—leaving symbols right in front of your eyes, embedded in everyday encounters. A hawk circles overhead during a moment of doubt. A feather appears on your doorstep after a night of grief. The same image or object keeps popping up—on your walk, in your feed, in a store window—until it demands your attention.

These manifestations are not random. They are messengers. The Universe often uses animals, objects, and patterns as tools for communication because they are immediate, visual, and rich with symbolism. You don't have to "believe" in omens or spirit animals to feel the uncanny power of these appearances. The point is not superstition—it's resonance. When something shows up again and again, especially with emotional charge or in moments of transition, it's not just decoration—it's a delivery.

This Chapter explores how the physical world becomes a stage for spiritual signs and how to recognize which messages are just noise and which ones are personal signals. When you begin to pay attention to recurring animals, symbolic objects, or repeated imagery, the world around you becomes less mechanical—and more enchanted.

Animal Messengers and Totemic Encounters

Since ancient times, humans have looked to animals as symbolic messengers. Indigenous cultures, mythologies, and spiritual systems from around the world have assigned meanings to animal encounters—not as fantasy, but as reflections of deeper truths. The idea is simple: animals, like numbers or dreams, carry archetypal energy. And when they appear in unusual ways—especially repeatedly—they are often mirroring something happening inside you or guiding your attention to something just beyond your current awareness.

Unlike seeing a dog while walking through a neighborhood filled with dogs, a true animal sign usually carries one or more of the following qualities: unexpected timing, repetition, emotional impact, or unusual behavior. For example, a fox crossing your path in a city where foxes are rare, or a butterfly landing on your hand during a moment of prayer, is not a common occurrence—it's a communication.

Each animal species tends to represent specific energies. While interpretations can vary by culture, here are some common themes:

- **Deer** often symbolize gentleness, grace, and the call to approach situations with soft strength.

- **Owls** are associated with hidden knowledge, intuition, and the need to trust inner vision.

- **Butterflies** represent transformation, letting go, and the emergence of a new self.

- **Ravens** can be signs of change, magic, or even messages from the spiritual realm.

- **Hawks or eagles** are often signs to zoom out, see from a higher perspective, and focus on purpose.

But the key to decoding animal signs isn't found in a list—it's found in how the animal makes you feel. What did you associate with it before this moment? What memories or emotions did it stir? What were you thinking about when the animal appeared?

Sometimes, the same animal will show up again and again across different forms—photos, dreams, live sightings, social media. That repetition is part of the message. The animal becomes a symbol in your personal mythology, a kind of spiritual avatar for a lesson, a phase, or a truth you're meant to embody.

You don't need to understand every encounter instantly. The goal is to acknowledge the experience, record your impressions, and remain open to the meaning unfolding over time.

Symbolic Objects and Found Messages

It's not only animals that carry messages. The Universe often uses objects—physical, tangible items—as messengers. These signs tend to show up in your environment at just the right time, delivering either comfort, validation, or direction. Some are traditional (like feathers, coins, or keys), while others are deeply personal, tied to a specific memory, person, or emotional theme in your life.

Consider the appearance of a white feather when you're grieving the loss of a loved one. Or finding an old key while contemplating a difficult decision. A found object can feel like a quiet miracle—something that shouldn't be there, but is, as if it were left for you. These signs are often deeply comforting, reminding you that you're not alone, that there's still order behind the apparent chaos.

Other symbolic objects might include:

- **Coins** – Often interpreted as signs of support, abundance, or affirmation that you are on the right path. The denomination or year might carry personal significance.

- **Keys** – Frequently symbolize access, opportunity, or new understanding. Finding a key during a moment of confusion can suggest that clarity is coming.

- **Rings or circular objects** – May represent unity, cycles, eternity, or closure. Appearing in moments of transition, they can signal the end of one Chapter and the beginning of another.

- **Mirrors or reflective surfaces** – These can be literal or metaphorical signs urging you to look within or reflect more honestly on a situation.

Sometimes, the object itself isn't the sign—it's what it reminds you of. An item might carry the energy of someone you've lost, or a phase of your life that's calling to be reintegrated. You might be guided to clean out a drawer and find something you forgot, just as you're dealing with a theme related to that period in your life.

The key with objects is not to become obsessive or over-interpret, but to feel for the **timing** and **context**. What are you facing? What question is alive in you? If an object shows up in alignment with those themes, it's more than decoration. It's guidance.

The Language of Repeating Patterns

Sometimes, signs don't arrive as specific animals or objects but as **patterns**—repeated symbols, shapes, or themes that echo across multiple areas of your life. You might start noticing spirals everywhere: in art, architecture, even your coffee foam. Or you keep hearing the same phrase from different people. Perhaps the number three begins showing up constantly—not just in clocks or prices, but in decisions you're facing: three choices, three invitations, three delays.

These patterns are not just coincidences. They form a kind of **energetic rhythm**—a theme the Universe is emphasizing because it reflects something essential about your current journey.

Repeating patterns often serve to:

- Draw your attention to something you've been avoiding.

- Affirm that you are moving in sync with your higher path.

- Trigger a realization that changes your perspective.

Patterns can be visual, verbal, numerical, emotional, or experiential. You might keep seeing bridges in photos and hearing metaphors about crossing over. That's not accidental—it's a symbolic download suggesting transition, connection, or decision.

The more you notice these patterns, the more intentional your life begins to feel. You begin to see threads weaving through your days, connecting one moment to the next in elegant, even mystical ways.

To work with patterns, keep a symbolic journal. Note when something repeats. Over time, the "coincidences" become a kind of narrative—a story the Universe is writing with you. And within that story are clues, insights, and moments of pure grace.

When the Universe Speaks Through Matter

The signs we seek are not only hidden in dreams or buried in emotion. They also walk beside us in the world of form—through animals, objects, and repeating motifs that echo our inner reality. These signs speak a visual, sensory language that bypasses logic and lands directly in the heart.

When you begin to treat the world as a field of living symbols, the mundane becomes magical. A feather is no longer just a feather. A fox is not just an animal. A series of threes is not just chance. These are touchpoints—gentle nudges from the intelligence that underlies everything.

You don't have to believe in omens to experience them. You only have to notice. To listen with your eyes. To walk through your day as if the world is trying to tell you something—because it is.

The more you pay attention, the more the signs appear. Not because they were never there, but because now, you're finally tuned in.

PART III: INTERPRETING THE MESSAGE

Chapter 9: The Language of Your Soul

One of the greatest misconceptions about signs from the Universe is that they speak in a fixed, universal code. That there's a single, correct meaning behind every number, animal, or coincidence. But in truth, signs don't arrive in a foreign language that you have to learn—they arrive in your language, using your memories, emotions, experiences, and symbolic associations to speak directly to you. The language of signs is the language of your soul, not someone else's.

That's why two people can see the same symbol and receive entirely different messages. A crow to one person might symbolize death or fear; to another, it may be a sign of magic or transformation. The deeper truth is that the Universe doesn't communicate through rigid definitions—it communicates through resonance. Signs are relational, not mechanical. They speak to the story you're living, the questions you're carrying, and the symbols that have meaning for you personally.

This Chapter explores how to recognize your soul's symbolic language, how to distinguish between borrowed meaning and authentic inner resonance, and how to build a living vocabulary of signs that evolves with you over time.

Your Inner Symbol Dictionary

Just like every individual has a unique fingerprint, each soul carries a personal library of symbolic associations. These are shaped by your upbringing, your culture, your traumas, your joys, your memories. A single symbol—like a rose, a train, or a bird—can carry vastly different meanings for different people based on how that symbol has been woven into their life story.

To understand the signs that show up in your life, you must begin to **translate them through your own lens.** What did that symbol mean to you before you started looking for signs? What memory does it bring up? What emotion rises when you see it?

For example, someone who grew up hearing their grandmother sing the same lullaby might later hear that melody in a store at a crucial moment in their life. That's not just nostalgia—it's communication. It's the Universe using a symbol already deeply encoded in the person's heart to deliver comfort, confirmation, or direction.

The same applies to visual symbols. Perhaps you always associated foxes with cleverness because of a childhood story. So when a fox crosses your path during a business dilemma, it doesn't just represent cunning in a general sense—it specifically connects you to a younger, sharper, more instinctual part of yourself that you may need to access.

Building your inner symbol dictionary takes time. It starts with noticing what symbols frequently appear in your dreams, memories, and meaningful life events. Journaling is a powerful tool here—especially when you track symbols not only in your external environment, but in your internal imagery, like dreams, daydreams, and sudden flashes of memory or inspiration.

Over time, patterns will emerge. Certain colors, shapes, songs, or numbers will start to feel loaded—not with anxiety, but with depth. These become your primary signs, your soul's native vocabulary. Once you recognize this personal dictionary, the signs become less confusing and more intimate. They no longer feel like mysterious puzzles. They feel like conversations you already know how to have.

Resonance over Rigid Interpretation

When you begin exploring signs, it's tempting to search for external definitions. You Google "spiritual meaning of 444" or flip through a dream dictionary. And while these resources can be helpful starting points, they're only half the story. The real question is not what a symbol means universally—but what it means to you right now.

That's where **resonance** becomes the deciding factor. Resonance is that felt sense of "this message is mine." It's not always logical. It's not always emotionally dramatic. But it carries a frequency you can feel—like a string inside you vibrates in response to the symbol. When you experience resonance, you're no longer just collecting data—you're receiving insight.

For example, let's say you see a white feather in the middle of the sidewalk. You could read a dozen interpretations online: messages from angels, peace, surrender, and so on. But none of that matters unless one of those meanings lands with you. Maybe, for you, white feathers remind you of a bird you had as a child. Or maybe they feel like a wink from a loved one who passed. Or maybe they simply show up whenever you're in a state of spiritual openness. That feeling—not the textbook definition—is the message.

The same goes for more abstract signs. Suppose you keep hearing the phrase "begin again." It pops up in a podcast, a book title, a conversation with a friend. Instead of assuming a generic meaning, pause and ask: Why does this feel important right now? Maybe you've been contemplating a career change but haven't admitted it out loud. Maybe you've been stuck in guilt or burnout. "Begin again" becomes more than a phrase—it becomes a key.

That's the power of resonance. It bypasses interpretation and becomes recognition. You don't need someone else to confirm it. Your body confirms it. Your heart does. That inner yes is the strongest compass you have.

To cultivate resonance, spend time sitting with the signs that show up. Don't rush to define them. Ask how they feel, where they take you emotionally, what memories they stir. The deeper you listen, the more clearly your soul begins to speak—and the more natural it becomes to trust that voice.

Evolving with Your Symbolic Vocabulary

Just as you grow and evolve, so does the language the Universe uses to reach you. Symbols that once felt meaningful may fade in relevance. Others may emerge, seemingly out of nowhere, to speak to new parts of your journey. This is a good thing. It means the dialogue between you and the Universe is alive.

For instance, you may go through a phase where you see butterflies everywhere—during a period of intense transformation. But once you've emerged from that cocoon, butterflies may stop appearing, and another symbol might take their place: bridges, rivers, or thresholds. The vocabulary has shifted to match your growth.

This is why it's so important not to cling to old meanings. A symbol that once meant "go forward" might later become a warning, or vice versa, depending on where you are emotionally, spiritually, and psychologically. The message is always dynamic. It reflects not just the symbol, but the context in which it appears.

This also means that your relationship with signs will deepen over time. At first, you may only notice external symbols—like numbers, animals, or objects. But eventually, you'll begin to pick up on more subtle signs: a sudden wave of clarity, a bodily sensation, an emotional shift that comes without explanation. These, too, are messages—spoken not through the outer world, but through your internal instrument.

You become the interpreter. Not by memorizing universal codes, but by becoming fluent in your own inner language.

Your task is not to master a system—it's to become more intimate with yourself. The more honestly you live, the more precisely the Universe can speak to you. Because in the end, the Universe isn't using some grand external cipher. It's using you—your history, your energy, your symbols—to reach the part of you that already knows.

The Language of Your Soul

The signs you seek will not always come in ways you expect. But they will always come in ways you can understand—if you listen through the lens of your own soul. The symbols that repeat, the images that linger, the words that echo—all of them are fragments of a language that belongs uniquely to you.

Trust your interpretations. Trust your feelings. Trust that the Universe is not speaking in riddles—it's speaking in your voice, using your life as the medium.

You don't need to look outside yourself to decode the messages. You only need to listen to the one who's always been listening back—your soul.

Chapter 10: Emotional Resonance: How It Feels Is the Clue

There's a subtle moment, often unspoken, that occurs when you experience a real sign. It's not necessarily what you see, hear, or read—it's what you feel. Not a mental "aha," but a quiet, often surprising emotional shift. It might come as a wave of peace, a jolt of excitement, or even tears welling in your eyes without clear reason. This is emotional resonance—the hidden tuning fork of truth vibrating within you.

We often ask, Is this a real sign or am I imagining it? But that's the wrong question. The better one is, How does it feel? The emotional tone of a moment is the most reliable indicator of its significance. Your body, heart, and energy field are wired to detect truth faster than your brain can rationalize it. Emotional resonance is what separates a passing coincidence from a meaningful message.

In this Chapter, we'll explore how emotion is the decoding mechanism for signs, how to distinguish true resonance from emotional noise, and how your body itself can become your most reliable spiritual instrument. When you learn to feel the message, you stop overthinking it—and start trusting it.

The Body as a Spiritual Antenna

Your body is not just a vehicle for experience—it's a sensing instrument, finely attuned to energetic information. Long before your conscious mind understands what's happening, your body is already responding. It tightens in fear, opens in joy, shivers in recognition. This is not superstition—it's biology. Your nervous system and your subtle energy field are constantly reading the world around you, including the invisible world of signs.

Think of a moment when you were deeply moved by something simple: a phrase someone said, a line in a song, an image that appeared just when you needed it. Maybe your skin prickled, or your breath caught, or tears formed unexpectedly. That wasn't "just" an emotion—it was your system saying, This matters. Pay attention.

The more tuned in you become, the more you'll notice that your body responds to symbolic moments without prompting. You may feel a flutter in your chest when you see a repeating number, or a sense of groundedness when you hear a certain word. These sensations aren't arbitrary. They are indicators of energetic alignment. They tell you that something has struck a chord—not just intellectually, but soul-deep.

This is why it's crucial to include your body in the process of interpreting signs. Don't just ask, What does this mean? Ask, How does this feel in my body? Where does the sensation land? Is there expansion or contraction? Ease or discomfort? These sensations are data—not just emotional, but intuitive.

Practicing this awareness turns your body into a trusted compass. Over time, you'll begin to differentiate between anxiety (tight, chaotic, urgent) and true intuitive resonance (clear, steady, calm—even when intense). The more you listen to the subtle shifts, the louder they become. Eventually, the body stops whispering and starts guiding.

Emotional Echoes and Lingering Clarity

Not all signs hit like lightning. Some are quiet but persistent. They leave what could be called an emotional echo—a feeling that lingers long after the sign has passed. You might forget the details, but the impression remains. That impression is often more important than the event itself.

For example, you hear a stranger mention a book that relates directly to your current life question. At the time, you smile, note the coincidence, and move on. But hours later, you're still thinking about it. You feel drawn to look up the book, or you find yourself journaling about the phrase they used. That's an emotional echo. The resonance didn't end with the event—it continued, which suggests that the sign had depth.

This lingering effect is one of the most trustworthy indicators that a moment was a true message. Your subconscious is still working with it, turning it over, absorbing it. The sign becomes not just a symbol but a seed—something that plants itself in your awareness and begins to grow.

Another clue is emotional contrast. Signs often show up during emotionally charged periods—uncertainty, grief, transition, longing. A true sign can shift the energy instantly. You might feel sudden calm in a storm of worry. Or spontaneous gratitude in a moment of fear. This shift is not random; it's resonance at work, adjusting your field.

Of course, not all emotional intensity is confirmation. Some reactions are rooted in trauma or memory, not meaning. The key is to observe what follows. Does the emotion deepen your sense of truth, or does it throw you into confusion? Does it feel clarifying or overwhelming? Resonance is often peaceful, even when it moves you to tears. It doesn't scatter your energy—it centers it.

Start noticing what sticks. What stays with you even after the moment passes? What you keep feeling is often more telling than what you felt for a moment. Real signs have emotional durability. They follow you—not to haunt you, but to remind you.

Discerning True Resonance from Projection

While emotional resonance is powerful, it must be tempered with discernment. Not every emotional reaction is a sign. Sometimes, we want a sign so badly that we read meaning into anything. We project our hope, fear, or fantasy onto a situation, and call it guidance.

This is where many people get stuck: confusing emotional charge with emotional truth. Wanting something to be a sign is not the same as it being one. Projection feels urgent, addictive, or obsessive. Resonance feels calm, complete, and grounded—even if it's surprising or challenging.

Here are some ways to differentiate projection from true resonance:

- **Projection is fueled by mental loops.** You keep analyzing the event, trying to "make it fit" your desired outcome. Resonance doesn't need justification—it just lands.
- **Projection feels unstable.** You swing between excitement and doubt. Resonance feels steady, even when subtle.
- **Projection is usually future-focused.** It attaches to what you want to happen. Resonance is rooted in the present. It brings awareness, not escape.

A useful practice when unsure is to wait and watch. True signs tend to repeat or clarify themselves over time. Projection fades when it's not fed. Give space. Let your body tell you what's real.

It also helps to check your emotional baseline. Are you grasping for control? Are you coming from fear or faith? The cleaner your emotional field, the clearer your resonance will be. This doesn't mean becoming emotionless—it means becoming emotionally honest.

Ultimately, resonance requires both openness and maturity. Openness to feel, receive, and trust. Maturity to reflect, pause, and not jump to conclusions. When these qualities combine, your emotional compass becomes incredibly accurate.

You won't just feel more—you'll feel more truthfully.

Emotional Resonance

Your emotional response is not an obstacle to spiritual insight—it is the insight. It's not the sign itself, but the inner vibration that tells you whether a moment is meant for you. The real confirmation doesn't come from external proof. It comes from how your body, heart, and soul respond.

When something is meant for you, you don't just understand it. You feel it. You recognize it. You don't need to force it or explain it to anyone else. The message lives in your bones. It echoes in your chest. It softens or stirs or awakens something that was sleeping.

The language of the Universe is emotional just as much as it is symbolic. And if you learn to listen with your feelings—not just your mind—you'll begin to trust the most reliable sign detector you have: your own heart.

Your next message may not come as a word or a vision. It may come as a feeling. One that says, without words: This is real. This is right. This is yours.

Chapter 11: False Positives: When It's Not a Sign (and You Want It to Be)

One of the most challenging aspects of working with signs is knowing when something isn't one. The more open you become, the more easily you notice symbols, synchronicities, and sensations. But with that increased sensitivity comes a potential trap: the tendency to project meaning where there isn't any—to see signs where none were given.

Wanting a sign can be a beautiful expression of longing and connection. But it can also become a subtle form of control, especially when the desire for clarity turns into a craving for confirmation. The heart wants to be reassured. The mind wants certainty. And in that vulnerable space, nearly anything—a glance, a number, a phrase—can be seized as validation.

This Chapter is about learning the difference between real spiritual communication and hopeful misinterpretation. It's about honesty, emotional sobriety, and building a stronger connection to truth, not just comfort. It's also about compassion—for yourself, for your seeking, and for the sometimes-messy process of learning how to listen well.

The Difference Between Desperation and Dialogue

It's easy to confuse emotional urgency with spiritual significance. When you're in distress or facing an unanswered question, you may find yourself unconsciously grasping at symbols, hoping that they'll deliver certainty or soothe anxiety. This is human and entirely understandable. But it can also cloud your discernment.

Desperation narrows perception. When you're desperate, you're not fully open—you're hunting for something to agree with what you already want. You may see a number sequence and immediately decide it's a green light, even if your gut is unsettled. Or you might hear a song lyric and declare it a divine message because it matches the narrative you're trying to believe, even if it goes against your better judgment.

A real sign, on the other hand, usually shows up when you're in a state of **receptive presence**, not emotional panic. It might still arrive during a difficult time, but your internal state when it lands is open, not grasping. You recognize it because it surprises you in some way. It cuts through the noise instead of confirming a script you wrote out of fear.

A helpful practice is to ask yourself: Am I seeking truth—or trying to avoid discomfort? This doesn't mean you should doubt every sign that makes you feel good. But it does mean you need to notice the difference between confirmation and projection. A true sign often brings peace, even when the message challenges your preferences. A false positive tends to bring adrenaline—but not clarity.

This is not about punishing your desire for meaning. It's about protecting your connection to real meaning, which doesn't need to be forced.

When the Mind Hijacks the Message

The human mind is a master storyteller. It can weave a narrative from nearly anything. And when the mind becomes overly active in the sign-seeking process, it tends to twist symbols into whatever serves its current agenda. This isn't malicious—it's self-protective. But it can lead you away from intuitive truth and into a maze of wishful thinking.

Here's what mind-hijacked sign reading often looks like:

- You constantly search for signs rather than allowing them to arrive organically.
- You reinterpret symbols until they match your desired outcome.
- You override your body's signals—such as unease or tension—because you want the external message to be true.
- You chase reassurance, not realization.

For example, you might be hoping to reconcile with someone who has distanced themselves. In your heightened emotional state, you start seeing their name everywhere, or hearing songs that remind you of them. Instead of checking how your body feels when you think of reuniting (perhaps tired, anxious, or ungrounded), you declare the signs proof that it's meant to be. You're not hearing the message—you're building a narrative.

That's not a conversation with the Universe. It's a performance directed by fear or longing.

To counter this, you need a different kind of awareness. One that doesn't eliminate emotion but includes it honestly. Try asking:

- Does this sign feel like a fresh insight or a justification?
- Would I still believe in this message if it pointed to a different outcome?
- Am I calm enough to hear a "no," or am I filtering for a "yes"?

When your ego lets go, the truth becomes audible. It may not tell you what you want to hear. But it will tell you what you need to hear. And that's the difference between self-soothing and spiritual alignment.

Practicing Discernment Without Fear

Once you realize that not everything you notice is a sign, it can trigger another kind of imbalance: hyper-skepticism. You start doubting everything. You become afraid to trust your intuition because you've seen how easily it can be influenced by emotion. This is just the other side of the same coin—trying to control the experience by denying it altogether.

Healthy discernment isn't cold or cynical. It's spacious, calm, and clear-eyed. It leaves room for magic and mistakes. It allows you to receive signs without grasping, and question them without shutting down. You're not looking for guarantees—you're looking for alignment.

To develop discernment without fear, you need to cultivate neutral observation. This means stepping back and noticing what you feel, without immediately labeling it as "the answer." Let the symbol be a symbol. Let the number be a number. Let your interpretation arise, not be forced.

A few grounding practices can help:

- **Wait for repetition.** One appearance may be noise. Three or more, in different forms, often signal a pattern worth noticing.
- **Check your baseline.** If you're exhausted, anxious, or triggered, give yourself time before interpreting anything.
- **Consult your body.** Resonance is felt. If the message is real, it will land with clarity—not confusion.
- **Stay open to paradox.** The sign might not mean what you expect. It may confirm one part of your intuition while challenging another. That's not failure—it's nuance.

One of the wisest things you can say to a possible sign is, Interesting. Let's see what else unfolds. That statement keeps the door open without pushing the process. It honors the experience without trying to control the outcome.

You don't have to be perfect at this. You're allowed to misread. You're allowed to want something so badly that you briefly believe in the illusion. But the more you practice, the more you'll recognize when you're leaning too hard, and when a message is leaning into you.

Spiritual maturity doesn't mean never making mistakes. It means learning how to tell when you're making one—and being gentle enough with yourself to correct course.

False Positives and Clear Knowing

It's easy to want every strange event or coincidence to be a sign. It gives comfort, structure, hope. But the true power of spiritual communication lies not in how often it occurs—but in how clearly it's heard. Not all moments are messages. Not all patterns are answers. And that's okay.

A false positive doesn't make you foolish. It makes you human. And your very desire to find meaning is a testament to your soul's longing to stay connected. Just remember: clarity never needs to be forced. When a sign is real, it lands. When it's not, you'll feel the effort it takes to keep believing in it.

Discernment is the gift that keeps your connection to the Universe clean. It ensures that when the real messages arrive—and they will—you'll be able to receive them with an open heart, an honest mind, and a quiet body that knows the difference.

Sometimes, the most honest sign is silence. And sometimes, the most loving answer is not yet.

Chapter 12: Anchoring the Message with Action

A sign, no matter how beautiful or mysterious, is ultimately meaningless if you don't do anything with it. While noticing, interpreting, and feeling signs are important, they are not the end goal. The point of receiving guidance from the Universe isn't just to feel seen—it's to be moved. Insight is the beginning, not the finish line. What transforms your life is what you do with the message once it's been received.

Anchoring a message means turning it into motion. It's about integrating spiritual insight into practical life—into choices, conversations, boundaries, and bold steps. Without action, signs remain symbolic. With action, they become tools of transformation. The Universe doesn't speak just to inspire you—it speaks to co-create with you.

This Chapter explores how to move from awareness to embodiment, how to act with alignment rather than fear, and how to ground the sacred into the real. If you've ever felt a sign deeply but didn't know what to do next, this is where clarity begins.

From Epiphany to Embodiment

It's easy to feel moved by a sign and then go right back to life as usual. You see 11:11 at the exact moment you're doubting a decision. You feel a wave of peace, take a deep breath—and then do nothing differently. This is common, and even understandable. Change can be scary. Insight without action is safe. But nothing changes until something changes.

The real magic of a sign is not in the recognition—it's in the response. The Universe sends messages not as commands, but as invitations. You're being invited to take a new step, shift your thinking, end a pattern, open a door. But the door won't open by itself. The symbol tells you there's a door. You still have to turn the handle.

To anchor a message, you must bridge the inner and the outer world. Ask yourself, What would this insight look like in action? If a dream told you to speak your truth, what's one real-life conversation you can have? If a repeating number suggested a new Chapter, what's one step you can take to close the old one?

Embodiment doesn't require grand gestures. Often, it begins with one small choice. Send the email. Say no where you used to say yes. Show up five minutes early instead of ten minutes late. Each aligned action becomes a signal back to the Universe: I'm listening. I'm participating. I'm ready.

When you move with the message, you shift from passive receiver to active co-creator. And that shift changes everything. Signs stop being abstract and start becoming alive in your body, your words, your day-to-day experience. That's embodiment. That's when spirituality becomes reality.

Action That Aligns, Not Reacts

It's important to note that not every response to a sign should be fast, loud, or dramatic. Acting on a message doesn't mean impulsively quitting your job or confronting someone at midnight. The kind of action that anchors a sign is rooted in alignment, not adrenaline. It's thoughtful, not frantic. Responsive, not reactive.

So how do you know the difference? Aligned action tends to feel clear, calm, and right, even if it stretches you. There's a steady inner yes that might come with nervousness but not confusion. Reaction, on the other hand, often feels desperate or urgent. It's a move to escape discomfort, not a move toward integrity.

Let's say you keep seeing symbols pointing you toward a creative project—maybe a book or business idea you've been avoiding. A reactive approach would be to announce your resignation tomorrow and try to build the whole thing overnight. An aligned approach would be to carve out consistent time for it, tell someone you trust, and start building the foundation slowly but seriously.

Similarly, if you receive a sign about a relationship—maybe a dream or synchronicity nudging you to reconnect or walk away—pause. Feel into it. Don't just act to relieve anxiety or validate a fantasy. Ask: What action would honor both the message and my highest self? Then take that step, even if it's quiet. Sometimes the most aligned action is simply telling the truth. Sometimes it's waiting a bit longer. Sometimes it's letting go.

The Universe doesn't rush you. But it does require that you meet it halfway. That means not ignoring signs out of fear, but also not grabbing them to justify impulsive moves. Real progress is made in small, rooted steps. One aligned action leads to the next. And over time, you'll look back and realize: you didn't just receive guidance—you walked it.

The Feedback Loop of Movement and Meaning

When you take action on a sign—no matter how small—you send a clear signal back to the Universe: I trust this process. I trust myself. And often, that single step opens the floodgates for more signs, more clarity, and more momentum. This is the feedback loop of co-creation.

A common mistake is to wait for all the signs before taking any action. But the system doesn't work that way. Often, you receive only the next sign, not the whole map. It's like walking through fog with a lantern. The light shows you a few feet at a time. But you only see more when you keep walking.

Every time you act with awareness, you activate the field around you. The Universe responds to movement. Synchronicities increase. Resources show up. People cross your path. This is not magical thinking—it's energetic alignment. When your inner reality and outer behavior match, you move into flow.

It's important to reflect on your results, too. After acting on a sign, ask yourself:

- How did I feel afterward?
- Did the path open or tighten?
- Did the next step become clearer or foggier?

This isn't about demanding instant outcomes. It's about tracking the conversation. Sometimes a sign leads to another layer of growth before the outcome appears. Sometimes the result is not what you expected, but better. Either way, movement creates feedback. And feedback refines your intuition.

You begin to trust your rhythm. You stop second-guessing every nudge. You realize that even if you misstep, you can course-correct. The path doesn't punish you for trying. It rewards you for showing up.

When signs become steps, and steps become a path, you are no longer just observing the magic—you're living it. You become someone who not only receives messages from the Universe but moves with them. And that movement becomes a kind of devotion—a physical prayer in motion.

Anchoring the Message

Signs are not there to decorate your life—they're meant to guide it. But guidance without action is like light without direction. Beautiful, but lost. The Universe meets you not just in your awareness, but in your willingness to move. When you embody the message—through choices, through changes, through small acts of courage—you make the intangible real.

Anchoring a message doesn't mean having it all figured out. It means letting the truth you received shape how you show up today. It means honoring the whisper with your next breath, your next step, your next yes or no.

If you've received a sign, the question now is: What are you going to do with it? What's the one small action that would turn the message into motion? You don't need to change your whole life overnight. But you do need to let it change something.

Because until you move, the message is only a possibility. Once you do, it becomes a beginning.

PART IV: CO-CREATING WITH THE UNIVERSE

Chapter 13: Turning Signs Into Strategy

Most people think of signs as magical or mystical—moments that guide, comfort, or surprise us. And they are. But signs are not meant to remain mysterious forever. Once you start to recognize, interpret, and act on them, they can become something far more powerful: a strategy. A sign is not just spiritual poetry—it can be practical guidance. It can become a compass for real-life choices, a tool for planning, and a way to make decisions with both intuition and structure.

Strategy is usually thought of as cold, rational, and deliberate. Signs are seen as emotional, intuitive, and unpredictable. But what if they're meant to work together? What if divine guidance is most effective when translated into an intelligent plan? When you take symbolic information and weave it into the architecture of your life—your goals, your work, your timing—you create a bridge between intuition and execution.

This Chapter is about using the signs you receive not just as comfort, but as data. Not just as a mystery to admire, but as a system to navigate. It's about transforming your spiritual insights into tangible strategies that can shape your decisions, relationships, career moves, and creative projects. Signs don't only appear to awaken your heart. They appear to direct your path.

From Intuition to Implementation

The moment you receive a meaningful sign, a decision follows. Will you act on it—or will you store it as a "nice idea" and move on? The first step toward turning signs into strategy is to stop treating them as isolated moments and start seeing them as part of a larger pattern.

One powerful way to do this is by tracking signs over time. Begin to document them—not just what you saw or experienced, but what you were feeling, what you were thinking about, and what was happening in your life. This builds a personalized symbolic map. Patterns emerge. Themes repeat. Certain symbols appear around similar questions or crossroads.

Once you identify these patterns, they become actionable insights. For example, if you consistently see butterflies during times when you're avoiding change, that's not just a metaphor—it's a cue. You can build it into your strategy: when the butterflies appear, ask yourself what you're resisting. That becomes a trigger for reflection and decision-making.

It also helps to define your intuitive "zones." These are areas of life where signs show up most clearly for you—relationships, creativity, health, money, transitions. Maybe dreams offer guidance around your emotional life, but number patterns guide your career.

Maybe animals show up during personal growth phases, while repeating phrases appear when you're considering travel or relocation. Noting these categories allows you to know where to look when you're navigating specific areas.

Then comes the key question: How do I act on this information in a structured way? That's where the bridge to strategy is built. Once you have clarity about what the sign is pointing toward, ask yourself:

- What's the next smallest, most practical step I can take?
- How can I create space in my schedule, resources, or mindset to follow this?
- What support or accountability do I need to carry this forward?

This is the implementation phase. It's where the insight becomes movement. You're not just admiring the message—you're building it into your life.

Designing a Life Around Alignment

Turning signs into strategy means aligning your external life with your internal compass. It's not about building a rigid plan and hoping the Universe approves—it's about creating a flexible plan that responds to real-time guidance.

Start by identifying areas in your life that feel stuck, misaligned, or overly forced. These are often zones where you've been making decisions from logic alone, or out of habit, fear, or obligation. Now ask: Have I been receiving signs here? Have certain messages, feelings, or synchronicities been pointing me in a different direction?

If the answer is yes, it's time to redesign that area of your life—not from scratch, but with intention. That might mean adjusting how you approach your work schedule, rethinking a relationship dynamic, or changing how you manage your energy.

For example, if you've been receiving signs that you need more solitude to recharge and refocus, you don't just reflect on that—you make it part of your strategy. You schedule time each week to unplug, say no to unnecessary engagements, and build your goals around sustainability, not burnout.

If you've received repeated nudges to pursue a creative idea, you don't wait for endless confirmation. You build time for it into your daily or weekly routine. You make the unseen seen by giving it structure.

This doesn't mean controlling every aspect of your life. Quite the opposite. It means living in **partnership** with guidance. You plan—but you leave space for adjustment. You move forward—but you stay alert to signs that ask you to pivot. Strategic living with signs is like sailing. You can set a course, but you must adjust your sails based on the wind.

The most aligned lives are not those that follow a rigid plan. They are those that make room for magic without losing direction. That's the sweet spot: structure plus synchronicity.

Signs as Metrics for Decision-Making

Strategy involves making choices—often hard ones. What to pursue. What to release. When to wait. When to leap. This is where signs can become practical tools, not just spiritual curiosities. You can use them as metrics—markers that help you test, affirm, or question your next move.

Here's how to start using signs to support decision-making:

1. Set a clear question. Vague requests create vague signs. If you're facing a choice, articulate the options. "Should I stay in this job or begin searching for something more aligned?" "Is this relationship helping or hindering my growth?"

2. Ask for confirmation. Not in desperation, but in partnership. "If moving toward this path is aligned, show me [specific sign] within [specific timeframe]." Be open, but specific enough to invite a clear signal.

3. Observe without obsession. Give the sign space to arrive. Stay present to how you feel while you wait. Sometimes the absence of a sign is a sign in itself.

4. Test through action. Don't wait forever. Take a small step toward the decision you're considering. See what unfolds. Does the path open or resist? Do new signs emerge? Your experience becomes part of the data.

5. Use the feedback loop. Continue to combine observation and movement. If you receive a green light, build on it. If you receive confusion, pause or reassess. Let the signs become part of your ongoing navigation system.

The key is not to become passive or obsessive. You're not outsourcing your power—you're using signs as collaborators in your growth. They offer information. You bring discernment, wisdom, and courage. Together, you make the next best decision.

When signs become part of your decision-making strategy, you gain something priceless: confidence. You're no longer making choices in a vacuum. You're in dialogue with something greater than yourself. And that dialogue brings both peace and power.

Turning Signs Into Strategy

Signs are not just moments of wonder. They are resources. They are data points in the system of your life. And when you gather them, interpret them, and implement them with clarity and integrity, they become part of your strategy—not just your spirituality.

Living strategically with signs means you stop waiting for everything to be certain. You begin listening for what's clear enough to act on now. You build momentum through small, meaningful steps. You adjust course with honesty and grace. And over time, your life begins to reflect your deepest values—not just in vision, but in structure.

You are not just being led. You are being equipped. And when you turn signs into strategy, you don't just receive magic—you create it.

Chapter 14: Living in Alignment with the Field

When you begin to notice signs, interpret them wisely, and take aligned action, something subtle yet powerful begins to shift. Life becomes less about effort and more about flow. You stop feeling like you're pushing a boulder uphill and start moving with an invisible current that supports, redirects, and occasionally astonishes you. This isn't just luck or intuition—it's the experience of living in alignment with the Field.

The Field is a term used across spiritual, scientific, and metaphysical traditions to describe the energetic matrix in which all things are connected. Some call it the quantum field. Others refer to it as the divine, Source, or universal intelligence. Regardless of the language, the idea is the same: there is a living, conscious fabric underlying reality, and when you align with it, life stops feeling random and starts feeling orchestrated.

This Chapter explores what it means to live in alignment with that Field—not just during moments of clarity, but as a sustained state of being. We'll examine how alignment manifests in daily life, what internal conditions support it, and how signs become more consistent and trustworthy when you live from this place of attunement.

What Alignment Really Feels Like

Alignment is not a constant state of bliss or perfection. It's not the absence of problems or pain. Alignment is a quality of connection—a felt sense that your inner world and outer actions are synchronized. It's when what you feel, know, and do are in harmony. When you are aligned, even challenges feel meaningful, because they're part of a larger rhythm that you can sense, even if you can't fully explain it.

The most common sensations people report when they're in alignment include clarity, peace, ease, creativity, synchronicity, and resilience. You begin to notice that things "click" more often. You're drawn to the right people, places, and ideas. Signs show up more regularly, and they don't feel like isolated miracles—they feel like part of the atmosphere.

Alignment also feels like presence. You're not spinning in anxiety or fantasizing about the future. You're here, awake, grounded. And because of that, you notice more. You move with more grace. You stop fighting every wave and start surfing the ones that are meant for you.

Importantly, alignment doesn't mean constant movement. Sometimes it feels like stillness, retreat, or silence. The Field doesn't value productivity above all else—it values coherence. And coherence sometimes means resting, healing, or simply waiting with trust.

If you've ever made a decision and then felt a quiet, full-body yes—that's alignment. If you've ever been in conversation and found the words coming through you instead of from you—that's alignment. If you've ever followed a hunch that led you somewhere better than logic could have—yes, that too.

These moments are not rare. They're reminders of your natural state. And the more you learn to return to that state on purpose, the more signs appear—not because you're lucky, but because you're available.

The Conditions That Support Alignment

Living in alignment with the Field doesn't happen by accident. It's not a matter of being chosen or gifted—it's a matter of attunement. Just like a radio must be finely tuned to receive a clear signal, your mind, body, and energy must be tuned to pick up on the flow of life.

There are certain internal conditions that tend to support alignment, and while they vary slightly from person to person, most include the following:

1. Honesty with Yourself

Alignment cannot coexist with self-deception. The more truthful you are with yourself—about what you want, what hurts, what's not working—the more aligned you become. Honesty clears static. It allows the Field to respond to the real you, not the version of yourself you're trying to maintain.

2. Emotional Regulation

Being in alignment doesn't mean never feeling strong emotions—it means not being run by them. When you can feel without collapsing, express without projecting, and move through fear instead of obeying it, you stay open. The Field speaks through subtlety. Emotional chaos drowns that signal.

3. Spaciousness

Too much noise—mental, physical, or digital—makes alignment harder. Quiet supports connection. Stillness creates receptivity. You don't have to become a monk, but you do have to create some room to breathe, reflect, and listen. Even ten minutes of daily silence can recalibrate your frequency.

4. Purposeful Attention

Where you put your attention matters. If you focus on scarcity, conflict, and fear, your experience narrows and contracts. If you focus on growth, beauty, and meaning, the Field seems to "respond" in kind—not because you've manipulated it, but because you've shifted your vibration. Attention is not just a cognitive tool—it's an energetic one.

5. Trust and Surrender

Perhaps the most difficult condition to cultivate is trust—especially when life is uncertain. But alignment requires a kind of soft confidence that says, I am guided, even when I don't see the whole path. When you trust, you relax. When you relax, you receive more. That doesn't mean you sit passively—it means you stop gripping and start dancing.

These inner conditions are not prerequisites for worthiness. You are always worthy of connection. But they are helpful practices—ways to become a better receiver, a clearer channel, a more conscious participant in the unfolding pattern.

Life Becomes a Dialogue, Not a Demand

When you live in alignment with the Field, life stops being something you push against. It becomes something you relate to. You stop demanding that everything go your way and start listening for how your way fits into the larger harmony.

This doesn't mean you lose your will or become passive. On the contrary, your intentions become sharper. You still make goals, take action, and speak desires—but you do so in conversation with the Universe, not in isolation from it. You begin to notice when life pushes back, and instead of forcing through, you inquire. Is this resistance or redirection? Am I in alignment or just attached?

Living in dialogue means staying responsive. You move when it's time to move. You rest when it's time to rest. You listen. You adjust. And because of this, you waste less energy. You stop solving problems that aren't yours. You stop chasing things that drain you. You start living more from the inside out.

This dialogue shows up everywhere—in synchronicities, in dreams, in gut feelings, in strange timing, in serendipitous meetings. The Field becomes an active participant in your choices. And you become an artist of timing, an intuitive strategist, a humble co-creator.

Even setbacks feel different when you're in dialogue. You stop asking, Why is this happening to me? and start wondering, What is this showing me? You don't collapse into despair. You lean into deeper questions. You stay connected, even when it hurts.

Over time, this way of living becomes second nature. Not because you never fall out of alignment—but because you know how to return to it. You become sensitive to your own signal. You recognize the static faster. You turn the dial, breathe, listen, and realign.

That's the secret of those who seem to "glow," who walk with grace, who live in seemingly effortless synchronicity. They are not exempt from confusion. They are just practiced at listening—and moving—from the inside.

Living in Alignment with the Field

Alignment is not a destination. It's a frequency. It's a way of being that you return to again and again—not because it's perfect, but because it's true. When you live in alignment with the Field, life becomes less like a battle and more like a song. You learn to hear the rhythm. You learn to follow the melody. You become a partner in a cosmic dance.

This isn't about escaping reality. It's about participating in it with deeper intelligence. It's about trusting that there's a wisdom beneath the surface—and living in a way that makes you available to that wisdom.

Signs are clearer when you're in alignment. Not because the Universe gets louder, but because you get quieter. You attune. You align. You move.

And in that movement, you become part of something much bigger than your plans—something that feels not only guided, but whole.

Chapter 15: Signs During Crisis, Change & Transition

It's easy to feel connected to the Universe when life is calm. When the signs are gentle and the path feels clear, everything aligns like a spiritual choreography. But what about when everything falls apart? What about the times when nothing makes sense, when the future vanishes behind fog, when grief, confusion, or fear are louder than your intuition? During these moments—periods of crisis, change, and transition—the signs don't stop. In fact, they often increase. But our ability to perceive them becomes clouded by pain.

This Chapter explores the role of signs during life's most difficult phases. Rather than being absent in the dark, the Universe often becomes more present. The signs shift in tone—not always playful or poetic, but anchoring, grounding, and deeply supportive. When your identity crumbles, when old maps stop working, and when you no longer recognize the shape of your life, these signs serve as lanterns in the fog. They don't solve everything, but they remind you: you are not alone. Something is still guiding you, even through the ashes.

Let's look at how signs appear in moments of rupture, what kind of messages are most common during major transitions, and how to remain open to guidance even when you're at your lowest.

The Nature of Signs in the Dark

Crisis has a way of stripping you down to your most essential self. Whether you're experiencing a breakup, job loss, illness, death, spiritual crisis, or major life pivot, the same disorienting truth emerges: the tools you used to navigate life before no longer work. It's here, in this raw place, that many people begin to search more earnestly for signs. And it's also here that the Universe often begins to speak more clearly—not necessarily louder, but deeper.

Signs in crisis tend to take on a different quality. They're not as playful or lighthearted. They often feel like quiet affirmations of your inner strength, breadcrumbs leading you one step at a time through uncertainty. A certain song plays right when you're about to give up. A dream brings clarity that your waking mind could not reach. A stranger's words resonate so precisely that you know you were meant to hear them.

In these moments, the signs are not just symbolic—they're stabilizing. They serve as handholds on a climb you didn't choose. You may not receive answers to every question. But you might receive enough to keep moving. Enough to take one more breath, one more step, one more choice in the direction of healing.

What's important to remember is that crisis changes how you perceive. The nervous system goes into survival mode. The mind races. The heart may close in self-protection. So it's not that the Universe goes silent—it's that your internal receivers get flooded. That's why signs in these moments often speak through the body and heart more than the intellect. They bypass mental chaos and land in emotional truth.

The more willing you are to soften—to let the pain be real but not final—the more you begin to feel the presence of something steady beneath the storm. A thread of guidance. A whisper in the noise. A strange peace that makes no sense, and yet holds you.

Signs That Accompany Transformation

During transition, you are shedding old skins. A version of you is dissolving—whether by choice or by force—and a new one has yet to emerge. This in-between space is fertile ground for signs, because your identity is less fixed. You're more permeable, more curious, more open to being shaped by forces beyond your ego. You may not know where you're going, but your soul does. And it's during these liminal phases that signs often arrive to confirm, encourage, and sometimes challenge you.

Common signs during periods of transformation include:

Recurring symbols in dreams — These often intensify during transition. You may repeatedly dream of crossing thresholds, packing or unpacking, changing clothes, navigating unfamiliar landscapes. These dreams are mirrors of the inner metamorphosis you're undergoing.

Uncanny timing and conversations — People may say things to you that feel too precise to be random. They may echo thoughts you've been carrying or speak directly to your fears. This kind of synchronicity is the Field responding to your evolving state, reminding you that life is aware of you.

Physical sensations and intuitive nudges — During change, you may feel strange bodily sensations that seem tied to decisions. Your chest may tighten around certain ideas or lighten around others. You might feel pulled toward a book, a location, a creative spark. These nudges are messages, too—embodied ones.

Symbolic objects appearing suddenly — Feathers, coins, animals, numbers, phrases, even billboards—any of these may arrive not just to get your attention, but to offer direction. For example, consistently seeing bridges might suggest you're in the process of crossing from one phase to another. Butterflies might confirm that your transition is sacred, even if messy.

One of the most difficult aspects of transformation is the ambiguity. You don't yet know what's being born. You only know what's dying. Signs in this phase don't always bring clarity about the end result—but they do bring presence. They say: Keep going. This matters. You're not broken—you're becoming.

It's essential not to rush through this phase. Let the signs accompany your process. Write them down. Reflect. Trust their accumulation, even if they don't immediately form a clear picture. The narrative will come. For now, your job is to stay open.

How to Stay Receptive in Pain

One of the great paradoxes of spiritual life is that signs often arrive most clearly when we are most broken—but we are also least likely to trust them. Pain makes you doubt. It makes you question your worth, your intuition, and your perception. You wonder if you're imagining things. You may even get angry at the Universe: Why didn't you stop this? Why aren't you helping more?

This emotional resistance is natural, but it doesn't have to close you off. There are gentle ways to stay receptive, even when your heart is aching.

1. Practice non-demanding attention.

Instead of begging for answers, simply stay curious. Say, I'm open to guidance today. I may not understand it, but I'm willing to notice. That small shift from demand to willingness makes a huge difference. It invites signs without attaching to them.

2. Soothe your nervous system.

Trauma and overwhelm create static. Breathwork, journaling, grounding, or simple acts of presence (like a walk, or even washing dishes slowly) can calm the noise enough to perceive subtle signals.

3. Ask small questions.

Instead of "What is the meaning of this entire crisis?" ask, What do I need today? What's the next right step? These questions are easier for the Universe to respond to—and easier for you to feel the answers to.

4. Honor the signs you do receive.

Even if a sign is small—a kind word, a strange coincidence, a feeling of peace—acknowledge it. Gratitude keeps the channel open. The more you validate the reality of these moments, the more they tend to increase.

5. Let yourself be held.

Ask for help—not just from the Universe, but from friends, therapists, mentors, or spiritual guides. Sometimes signs come through other people. And sometimes, love itself is the message.

You don't have to be spiritually "on" during crisis. You don't have to interpret everything correctly. You don't have to be grateful for your pain. You simply have to stay in relationship with the possibility that you are not alone in it. That something greater still walks with you, even through the shadow.

Signs in Times of Change

Crises break us open—but that opening makes space for something deeper. And in that space, the Universe often speaks with surprising intimacy. The signs you receive during hard times may not fix your problems, but they remind you that your pain is witnessed, your growth is sacred, and your path is not an accident.

Change is the crucible where the old dissolves and the new is born. Transition is not a failure of stability—it's an invitation to trust what you cannot yet see. And the signs that appear in these moments are not just messages. They are companions. They are quiet evidence that something intelligent is still holding your story.

You don't have to know the destination to take the next step. You just have to notice the light that flickers at your feet, trust that it means something, and walk—one moment at a time—into the unfolding mystery of who you are becoming.

Chapter 16: How to Ask for (and Receive) Clearer Signs

There comes a point in the journey when you're not just waiting for signs to arrive—you want to cooperate with them. You want to open a two-way dialogue with the Universe, to stop feeling like a passive recipient and start becoming a conscious participant in the conversation. That's where the art of asking for signs comes in—not pleading or manipulating, but requesting with clarity, humility, and trust.

Asking for signs isn't about forcing the Universe to give you what you want. It's about opening a channel, sharpening your awareness, and inviting guidance to meet you in your current state. And when done with sincere intention, the results can be extraordinary—not because the Universe finally decides to help, but because you finally become able to hear it more clearly.

In this Chapter, we'll explore how to ask for signs in a grounded, spiritually aligned way. We'll look at how to frame your request, how to recognize the response, and what to do when signs seem absent or ambiguous. Clear signs often follow clear intentions—and learning to ask well is a powerful step toward living in conscious partnership with the invisible intelligence guiding your path.

The Intention Behind the Ask

Before you even formulate your question, pause and check your motivation. Why are you asking for a sign? Are you seeking guidance—or permission? Are you trying to bypass a decision—or deepen your understanding of it? Are you coming from fear, uncertainty, longing, faith?

The intention behind your request shapes the kind of response you're likely to receive—or perceive. When you ask from a space of desperation, you may be more prone to false positives or projected meanings. When you ask from curiosity, reverence, and presence, your perceptual field expands, and real signs can enter more easily.

You don't need to be perfect or enlightened to ask for a sign. You simply need to be honest. A heartfelt, unpolished request like "I don't know what I'm doing. Please show me the way" can be more powerful than a perfectly worded spiritual petition.

That said, clarity helps. The more specific your question, the easier it is to notice a relevant answer. For example, instead of saying, "Show me a sign if I'm on the right path," you might say, "If staying in this relationship serves my growth, please send me a clear symbol in the next 48 hours—one I will unmistakably recognize." This doesn't demand control. It offers a framework. It gives the Field something to work with.

You can also choose a sign in advance—a symbol you're open to receiving. Maybe you say, "If this job opportunity is in alignment, let me see a blue butterfly." The point isn't to be arbitrary. The point is to establish a shared code that you and the Universe can work with. Just be sure that the symbol you choose is unusual enough that its appearance will feel meaningful.

Above all, speak your request out loud—or write it down. The act of articulating it anchors the energy. It moves the question from the mental realm into the energetic one, where it can begin to interact with the field around you.

Recognizing the Response

Once you've asked for a sign, you enter the space of listening. This is the most delicate and potent part of the process—not passive waiting, but active receptivity. You're not just hoping for a message to appear; you're paying attention to how life begins to echo your question.

Clear signs can arrive through virtually any medium: numbers, animals, overheard conversations, song lyrics, books, dreams, chance encounters. The key is not to interpret every flicker of reality as a sign but to feel for resonance. You'll know a message is meant for you because something inside you recognizes it. You'll feel seen, stirred, or strangely clarified. The timing will be too sharp, the symbol too specific, the emotional impact too deep to ignore.

Here are a few things to notice as you wait:

1. Repetition

A clear sign often appears more than once—especially if you miss or dismiss it the first time. If you asked for guidance and suddenly see the same word, symbol, or theme show up in three unrelated places within a day or two, pay attention. Repetition is one of the Universe's favorite delivery methods.

2. Emotional weight

Not all signs feel profound, but the ones that carry meaning usually shift your inner state. You might feel peace, courage, joy, or a softening in your heart. Even if the sign isn't what you hoped for, it tends to bring clarity rather than confusion.

3. Precision

Sometimes, a sign hits with such precision that it feels surgical. A line from a movie echoes your unspoken question. A stranger mentions your exact dilemma. A dream gives you an answer in metaphor so clear it can't be coincidence. These moments aren't about drama—they're about unmistakable personal relevance.

4. Disruption

A real sign may interrupt your assumptions or plans. It might not tell you what you want to hear. But if it's truth-based, it will free you—even if it initially discomforts you. Don't ignore a sign just because it asks you to grow.

It's also possible that the sign you receive comes in a way you didn't expect. You might ask for a red rose and instead get a dream about your grandmother holding one. Or you might ask to see a specific animal and instead hear someone talking about it in line at a coffee shop. Don't be too literal. The Field is creative. Trust how the symbol arrives—and how it lands.

Most importantly, give it space. Don't fixate. Ask, then release. Go about your day with a quiet openness. Let the message arrive when and how it wants to.

What to Do When No Sign Appears

One of the most frustrating spiritual experiences is asking sincerely for a sign and receiving… nothing. No dream. No symbol. No surge of clarity. Just silence.

But silence, too, is a form of communication. It doesn't mean you've been ignored. Often, it means:

- You already know the answer, and the Universe is waiting for you to act.
- Your request wasn't aligned (e.g., seeking control, escape, or validation).
- You're not yet ready to receive the answer, emotionally or energetically.
- The timing isn't right—other pieces are still falling into place.
- The sign is arriving in a form you're not recognizing.

Instead of taking the absence personally, use it as an opportunity to realign. Ask a different question. Widen your awareness. Get quiet and revisit your emotional state. Are you asking from trust—or from panic? Are you listening for truth—or filtering for what you want to hear?

Another helpful step is to pause and reflect on what's already been given. Sometimes we miss signs because we're looking for new ones while ignoring the old ones. Ask yourself:

- What signs have I already received that I've doubted or dismissed?
- What's the message I keep hearing but don't want to face?
- What do I already know—but haven't yet acted on?

You can also ask for clarification. Say, "If that last sign was real, please confirm it in a different way. Show me something else that reinforces the message." The Universe doesn't tire of your sincerity. It responds to your engagement.

In the meantime, don't stop living. Signs love motion. Often, it's when you're immersed in something meaningful—walking, creating, helping someone, even laughing—that the clearest signs appear. Why? Because your energy is open, curious, flowing. That's when the signal gets through.

Trust is the bridge between asking and receiving. When you trust, you stay open. You don't freeze in doubt. You remain available to be met—not just by symbols, but by synchronicity, by people, by paths opening unexpectedly.

And even when signs are few, remember: the absence of a sign is not the absence of support. Sometimes, your trust is the sign.

How to Ask for Clearer Signs

Asking for a sign is not a magical formula. It's an act of intimacy. It's saying to the Universe: I'm listening. I'm willing. Show me what I need to see. And that willingness changes the energy. It invites meaning to move toward you.

When you ask with clarity, receive with humility, and trust with consistency, you enter into sacred dialogue. You stop guessing. You start relating. You become someone who no longer waits passively for direction—but actively co-creates it, moment by moment.

So ask. Ask with your voice, your breath, your journal, your longing. And then step back and let the Field respond. It will. Maybe not always on your schedule. Maybe not always in the form you expect. But always, in some way, it will answer.

Because the Universe is not silent. It's listening for you to speak first.

PART V: THE PATH BEYOND THE SIGNS

Chapter 17: Signs as Training Wheels

At the beginning of your spiritual or intuitive journey, signs feel like lifelines. They reassure, guide, and orient you when you feel lost or uncertain. They validate that something larger is listening, caring, and communicating. But as your awareness deepens, you'll likely reach a point where the signs begin to shift in meaning. You begin to wonder if you still need them in the same way—or if they've simply been tools to help you strengthen something within yourself.

Just like training wheels on a bicycle, signs are incredibly helpful when you're first learning how to balance. But at a certain point, balance becomes internalized. You ride not because the wheels are holding you up, but because you've developed the skill of movement. Similarly, signs are there to help you notice the invisible, but not to replace your inner knowing. They are invitations to build trust in your own connection to life.

This Chapter explores the transition from dependence on signs to integration of the wisdom they point toward. It's about what happens when you begin to embody the message instead of constantly seeking external confirmation. It's not about leaving signs behind, but about evolving your relationship with them—from reliance to resonance, from needing proof to simply knowing.

The Purpose Signs Serve Early On

In the early stages of intuitive awakening, the world can feel chaotic, uncertain, and even frightening. You begin to question things you once accepted. You may be shedding beliefs, relationships, and goals that no longer align with your evolving self. During this vulnerable time, signs can act as grounding forces. They show up like gentle affirmations: you're not alone, you're on the right track, you're seen.

These early signs are often vivid, repeated, and emotionally potent. They might appear as animals crossing your path, numbers that follow you everywhere, or dreams that seem far too specific to be random. For many people, these signs are the very events that initiate their spiritual awakening. They awaken a sense of wonder, a feeling of being in conversation with life. And in this phase, that wonder is essential. It cracks open the shell of skepticism and softens the walls of habitual thinking.

Signs also build trust. When you ask for guidance and receive a response, you begin to believe that you're supported. When you follow a sign and it leads to a beneficial outcome, you begin to trust your intuition. This is not superstition or blind faith—it's experiential learning. You see the connection between your inner state, your questions, and what appears in the world around you. That realization builds a foundation of spiritual confidence.

Eventually, though, something begins to shift. You notice that you're receiving fewer signs, or that they don't carry the same emotional charge they once did. This can be unsettling at first. You may wonder if you've lost your connection or if something's wrong. But more often than not, this shift means something is right. It means you're evolving into a new phase where external signs are no longer the primary source of guidance—they've done their job, and now the wisdom they awakened is becoming part of you.

Trust as an Internal Compass

As your relationship with signs matures, you start to notice that guidance doesn't always come from outside. It begins to rise from within—from a sense of deep inner knowing that doesn't need validation to feel true. You make decisions not because you saw a feather float across your path, but because your body, heart, and intuition align in quiet agreement. This is the transition from being led by signs to being led by trust.

This trust is not arrogance or recklessness. It's not ignoring signs—it's integrating them. It's knowing that the same intelligence that sends messages through the world also lives inside you. And that you don't need to constantly seek permission from the Universe to follow your truth. You begin to walk in partnership with it, not dependence on it.

In this phase, your inner compass becomes more sensitive. You feel subtle shifts in your energy when something is or isn't aligned. You don't need three repeating numbers to tell you to leave a draining job—you can feel it in your body. You don't need a bird to fly in front of your car to remind you to slow down—you already noticed your nervous system tightening.

This doesn't mean signs disappear altogether. In fact, they may still appear, but you recognize them differently. They're less about course correction and more about resonance. They confirm what you already feel. They don't initiate movement; they echo it. And that's the key: you're not waiting for life to move you—you're already moving in alignment, and life reflects that.

Building trust in your own inner knowing takes time, and it doesn't mean you won't occasionally doubt or ask for confirmation. But you begin to feel that you are the channel, not just the receiver. You are part of the field, not separate from it. And that knowing becomes the compass you carry into every room, every decision, every change.

When to Let Go—and When to Still Listen

Knowing when to let go of sign-seeking is a subtle art. It doesn't mean rejecting signs or pretending you're above them. It means discerning when you're using signs to avoid responsibility rather than deepen your presence.

There are moments when asking for a sign is appropriate, empowering, and even necessary—particularly when you're overwhelmed, confused, or at a major life crossroads. But there are also times when asking for signs becomes a way to delay action. When you already know what needs to be done, but you keep asking for more signs to avoid doing it.

Letting go of this habit is an act of maturity. It's saying to the Universe, I trust that you've given me enough to move. I trust myself to take the next step, even if it feels uncertain. That step becomes your new sign. Your own movement becomes the message.

Still, you never fully stop listening. You simply refine how you listen. You stop asking for constant external proof and begin attuning to your internal resonance. You recognize that the most powerful sign is how a decision feels in your heart, how it settles in your body, how it aligns with your deepest values.

And yet, signs still come. Often when you least expect them. They arrive not because you need them to make a choice, but because they are part of the poetic intelligence of life. A white feather lands at your feet on the day you forgive someone. A hawk flies overhead just as you speak your truth. A stranger says the exact words you needed to hear.

You smile, not in dependence but in recognition. You didn't need the sign. But it came anyway. Like an old friend nodding from across the room—not because you needed directions, but because you were already walking in the right direction.

Signs as Training Wheels

Signs are beautiful, mysterious, and life-affirming. They remind us that we are not alone, that we are part of a larger conversation, that life is listening. But they are not meant to keep us dependent. Their deeper purpose is to awaken our own inner guidance—to teach us how to feel, trust, and move without needing constant confirmation.

At some point, the signs become less like instructions and more like background music—pleasant, meaningful, affirming, but not necessary for every step. You're no longer checking the sky for messages every hour. You're simply living the message. Walking the truth. Becoming the sign.

You'll always be connected. You'll always be part of the field. But now, instead of chasing signs, you carry their essence with you. And that is freedom. That is maturity. That is the moment when spirituality becomes embodiment.

So ride with the training wheels. Lean on signs. Let them guide you. But trust that a day will come—perhaps sooner than you think—when you realize: the sign you've been waiting for... is you.

Chapter 18: Becoming the Sign for Others

There's a point in every seeker's path where the focus begins to shift. At first, the journey is deeply personal. You search for signs, follow inner callings, and heal long-carried wounds. You build trust in your intuition and learn to co-create with the Universe. But as your connection deepens, you realize something unexpected: you're not only here to receive signs—you're here to become one.

Becoming the sign for others doesn't mean you have all the answers or that you play the role of some enlightened guide. Rather, it means living in such integrity and presence that your life radiates alignment. You become a mirror, a reminder, a spark—often without even trying. Your story, your energy, your kindness, your courage to live truthfully can become the very sign someone else was praying for.

This Chapter explores how we each have the capacity to become signs for others, not through perfection or performance, but through our willingness to embody what we've learned. It's about recognizing the ripple effect of authenticity, and how your life, lived fully and openly, can become a kind of silent transmission—one that touches lives in ways you may never fully realize.

Your Presence as a Message

The most profound signs often aren't dramatic—they're embodied. They show up in people whose very way of being offers clarity, comfort, or inspiration. Maybe it's the teacher who listens without judgment, the stranger who offers a timely word, or the friend whose resilience reminds you of your own. We remember these people not because they had the right answers, but because their presence made something true inside us feel more accessible.

You don't need to be loud or spiritual or wise to carry this kind of impact. What matters is that your presence is aligned. When you are at peace with yourself, others feel safer being themselves. When you are kind without motive, others remember that goodness exists. When you speak your truth with softness, you give others permission to do the same.

In this way, you become a living message—not because you try to be, but because who you are radiates what others need to remember. You become a living symbol of possibility, especially in a world where many are still searching for their own center.

Think about the people who've been signs in your life. Chances are, they weren't trying to "teach" you anything. They were simply showing up as themselves—whole, honest, or vulnerable in a way that pierced your heart open. That's what presence does. It cuts through noise and awakens something deeper.

You don't need to be perfect to have this impact. In fact, your imperfections are often what connect you to others most. When you share your story—not the polished version, but the real one—you offer others a bridge from shame to healing. When you model forgiveness, patience, or courage in your daily choices, you help others believe that those qualities are possible for them, too.

So don't underestimate the impact of simply being yourself, fully and unapologetically. Your presence may be the sign someone else has been waiting for.

Acts That Create Ripples

Sometimes we are the sign not through who we are, but through what we do. A gesture, a word, a message delivered at just the right time—these become catalytic moments in someone else's journey. What seems small to us can feel like divine intervention to another.

The beauty of this is that you don't always know you're being a sign. You may write a sentence that sticks in someone's mind for years. You may give a compliment that reroutes someone's self-worth. You may help someone carry groceries, and it shifts their belief in the kindness of strangers. These moments matter.

Becoming the sign in this way means acting with awareness, even in ordinary life. It's asking, What energy am I bringing into this space? What opportunity for kindness or presence is in front of me right now? You don't have to go looking for people to save. Just stay awake to the fact that every interaction is an opportunity to reflect truth, love, or clarity.

Here are some simple ways acts can become signs:

- **Offering encouragement without expectation.** A single sentence of support, spoken at the right moment, can carry someone through weeks of doubt.

- **Sharing your story vulnerably.** When you tell the truth about your own journey, you create space for others to be honest about theirs.

- **Following your intuition publicly.** When you take a leap of faith and own it, others watching may feel empowered to take theirs.

- **Listening deeply.** In a world of distraction, genuine listening is healing. Being fully present for someone can be a sign that their voice matters.

- **Making aligned choices.** When people see you make decisions from integrity rather than fear or conformity, they begin to believe that they can too.

Many people are praying for a sign—and often, it arrives in the form of another human being showing up with love, with truth, with courage. You may be the person who nudges them back toward themselves. And you don't need to know that you've done it. The ripples will move through the world with or without your awareness.

Holding Space Without Interfering

It's tempting, once you realize you can be a sign for others, to try to become one deliberately. But this usually backfires. The most powerful influence we have comes from living truth, not preaching it. If you try to play the role of a guide or healer without being invited, you may end up projecting instead of empowering.

Becoming the sign means being available, not invasive. It's about holding space, not taking control. Trust that others are on their own journey—and that they will see what they're ready to see, when they're ready to see it. Your job is not to deliver their lesson. Your job is to embody your own.

Sometimes, being the sign means staying silent when you want to speak. Sometimes it means offering compassion instead of advice. Sometimes it means walking away from what drains you so that your life can be an example of boundaries and self-respect.

When you live in integrity, others feel it. When you make space for your own intuition, others feel more invited to explore theirs. And when you walk in trust—not needing to fix or convert—you allow the field of transformation to open around you. People can feel that. They may not even know why, but something in them shifts.

This kind of presence creates a spaciousness that allows others to hear their own truth more clearly. That's the paradox: the more you try to be the sign, the less effective you become. The more you live the truth, the more naturally you radiate the signal.

So be the sign not by trying, but by tuning yourself. Stay close to your own alignment. Trust that your being, not your effort, is what speaks most powerfully.

Becoming the Sign for Others

You came to this journey looking for signs. You followed them, questioned them, learned their language. Now, without even realizing it, you've become part of that language. Your life, lived with sincerity, presence, and courage, is its own form of communication.

You don't have to be famous or wise or enlightened to matter. You simply have to be real. To live in such a way that your presence reminds others of their own light. To walk through the world with enough softness that others feel safe, and enough clarity that others feel inspired.

This is the great loop of guidance: what you once needed, you now carry. What once felt like a whisper from beyond now flows through you. You are not just a seeker of signs. You are a living one.

And someone, somewhere, may look at your life, your smile, your resilience, your truth—and without even knowing why, take a deep breath and say, There it is. That's the sign I needed.

Chapter 19: The Feedback Loop of Faith

At some point, the journey of recognizing and following signs becomes something deeper than guidance. It becomes a relationship—an ongoing exchange between your inner state and the field around you. And at the heart of that relationship is one element more transformative than any symbol, number, or synchronicity: faith.

Faith is not blind belief. It's not a refusal to question or doubt. It's an active trust that something meaningful exists beneath the surface, even when you can't see it clearly. It's the willingness to keep listening, acting, and showing up in alignment, even when the signs are subtle, the answers delayed, or the outcome unknown.

In this Chapter, we explore the energetic loop between belief and perception—how what you believe shapes what you see, and what you see reinforces what you believe. This is the feedback loop of faith. It isn't a trick of positive thinking or a mystical loophole. It's a living dynamic between you and the universe, in which your inner trust cultivates outer evidence, and that evidence deepens your inner trust. The more you believe that life is communicating with you, the more clearly it seems to do just that.

Belief Shapes Vision

The world you experience is not just shaped by what's happening outside of you—it's filtered through your expectations, perceptions, and attention. This is not about delusion or fantasy. It's about orientation. Two people can walk through the same day and experience it entirely differently, depending on what they're attuned to.

If you expect the world to be hostile, you notice every slight. If you believe the universe is indifferent, you miss the subtle invitations toward connection. But if you believe, even tentatively, that something intelligent and supportive is woven into the fabric of life, your eyes begin to search for evidence—and they tend to find it.

This isn't magical thinking. It's neurology. The brain's reticular activating system (RAS) is wired to filter reality according to what you've decided is important. When you tell yourself, "I am supported, and I'm open to signs," your RAS begins to prioritize inputs that reflect that belief. Suddenly, the world doesn't just seem more meaningful—it is more meaningful to you, because your consciousness is shaping what comes into focus.

Faith activates this perceptual lens. It says, "I may not see it yet, but I trust it's there." That trust doesn't make signs appear out of nowhere. It makes you receptive to noticing what's already been trying to reach you.

Faith expands your reality. It stretches your vision beyond survival and repetition and into co-creation. It doesn't require proof before belief. It starts with belief, and then allows proof to emerge—not as a reward, but as a natural result of changed perception.

The Loop in Action: How Trust Deepens Clarity

Once you begin to believe that life is interactive—not random, not chaotic, but participatory—you create the conditions for a feedback loop. Your openness invites signals. The signals reinforce your trust. The trust makes you more open. And on it goes, deepening each time you engage with it consciously.

This is why small experiences of connection matter. They form the early feedback—just enough to keep you going. Maybe you ask for a sign and receive one within hours. That moment lights a spark in your awareness. You say, "That was real." That conviction subtly shifts your orientation. You notice more. You feel guided more often. And as a result, you begin to rely less on constant reassurance and more on inner alignment.

Faith is strengthened not by having everything go your way, but by staying connected through the unknown. The loop doesn't require certainty. It requires presence. Every time you act from intuition, even without confirmation, and it leads to a better outcome—or even just to peace—you're feeding the loop. You're building evidence that trust works. Not because it guarantees control, but because it aligns you with the deeper rhythm.

Conversely, when you act out of fear or distrust, and the result brings chaos, that too is part of the loop. It teaches you what misalignment feels like. It sharpens your inner compass. Eventually, you learn that clarity is not something you wait for passively. It's something you generate by walking in alignment—even when it's uncomfortable, even when it's slow.

The more you engage with the loop, the more subtle your sensitivity becomes. At first, you needed obvious signs—loud synchronicities, repeating numbers, clear dreams. Now, you begin to feel guidance in quieter ways. A whisper in your chest. A lightness when you speak your truth. A strange certainty with no logical source.

You no longer need dramatic confirmation to move. Your body becomes a barometer. Your soul becomes the map. The loop has internalized.

From Seeking Signs to Living in Alignment

Faith doesn't mean you stop seeking guidance. It means the nature of your seeking changes. You don't need the universe to constantly intervene with signs to prove that you're on the right track. You begin to live in a way that makes signs inevitable—because you are living in resonance.

This shift is subtle but profound. In earlier stages, signs help you decide. You ask for a sign to validate a choice. You hesitate, waiting for something to push you forward. But over time, that waiting begins to feel unnecessary. Not because signs no longer matter, but because you've learned to read yourself.

Now, you make choices based on inner congruence. You notice whether your decisions feel aligned with your values, your energy, your purpose. And when a sign comes, it doesn't tell you what to do—it affirms what you already felt. You're not looking for external permission. You're looking for confirmation that your inner compass is still on point.

This is the mature phase of the feedback loop. You're not operating from insecurity, hoping the universe will correct you. You're walking with trust, knowing that if you veer off-course, you'll feel it—and the universe will nudge you gently back.

Living in alignment doesn't mean you're always certain. But it means you're no longer afraid of uncertainty. You trust that you'll be shown what you need, when you need it. And until then, you live your questions with grace.

This is when signs become more like echoes than instructions. You act from faith, and reality resonates in response. You take a leap, and the net appears—not because you demanded it, but because you trusted enough to jump.

You stop wondering, "What if nothing is guiding me?" and start knowing, "Something always is—even when it's quiet."

The Feedback Loop of Faith

Faith is not a one-time decision. It's a practice. It's a choice you make every day—to trust the unseen, to honor the subtle, to keep walking even when you can't yet see the road. And the more you choose it, the more reality reflects it back to you.

This is the feedback loop of faith: you trust, and your trust sharpens your vision. Your vision confirms what you trusted. And slowly, this loop becomes your baseline. Not because you have all the answers, but because you've stopped needing constant proof.

The world hasn't changed. You have. And in changing, you've altered your relationship with reality itself. You now move not as someone trying to get signs, but as someone living from the same frequency that creates them.

You're not chasing guidance. You're walking with it.

The signs you used to seek so desperately now arrive like gentle echoes—sweet, surprising, and affirming. But you no longer need them to move. You're already moving. You're already aligned. And in that movement, the Universe whispers, Yes. Keep going.

Chapter 20: Your Reality Is Speaking. Always.

The journey we've taken through this book began with the idea that signs are rare, precious, and perhaps reserved for certain moments of divine intervention. But as your perception deepens, that initial assumption begins to unravel. Signs are not exceptions to the rule of life—they are the rule. The Universe doesn't whisper guidance only when you beg for it. It's speaking all the time, through every layer of reality, in ways that are personal, symbolic, and alive.

This Chapter is both an ending and a beginning. It's a reminder that the signs you've learned to notice are not just scattered messages along your path. They are the path. Every moment—whether it feels sacred or mundane—holds within it a potential signal. Whether through symbols, emotions, coincidences, or subtle inner cues, reality is constantly responding to you, reflecting you, guiding you.

We'll explore how to maintain this awareness beyond the final page of a book. We'll look at how to make your life a living dialogue, how to spot the signals hidden in the ordinary, and how to sharpen your trust in the conversation that never ends.

Every Moment Contains a Message

The idea that reality is responsive isn't just poetic—it's energetic. Every thought, feeling, and action you emit has a frequency, and reality meets that frequency in kind. This doesn't mean every event is your fault or that you're manifesting every challenge. Rather, it suggests that how you show up affects what you notice and how you experience what happens. Your awareness, then, becomes the tuning dial.

When you're fully present—even in the smallest moments—you begin to feel that nothing is random. The way a stranger looks at you. The moment your favorite song plays. The way your body feels when you say yes to something. These are not accidents. They are threads in the living web of signs.

If you pay close attention, you'll notice that reality often speaks in repetition. You'll hear the same phrase from different people in the same day. You'll see an image show up in dreams, media, and the street. You'll get a feeling in your gut that something is coming—and then it does. This consistency is not illusion. It's the mark of pattern, presence, and precision. It's the way the Field reminds you: I'm still here. Are you still listening?

Even pain contains messages. Resistance in your body, chaos in your circumstances, recurring emotional triggers—these, too, are signs. Not punishments, but signals. They say, "Look here. Something wants your attention. Something wants to be seen, released, changed."

By accepting that every moment holds the potential for meaning, you stop searching for magic outside yourself. You start finding it right where you are—in traffic, in conversation, in solitude, in conflict. You start treating life as a mirror, not a maze.

This shift doesn't make life easier, but it makes it richer. It means you are never disconnected. The conversation is never over. And you are never without guidance—only without awareness.

Living in Daily Dialogue

When you view reality as responsive, your relationship to the world becomes interactive. You don't just experience life—you engage with it. You listen, question, respond, and reflect. You create feedback loops not just with people, but with time, space, and energy itself. Life becomes a living, breathing conversation.

This way of living is not about being hyper-vigilant or obsessively decoding every detail. It's about being available to meaning, without grasping for it. You walk through the world like a poet—noticing what others overlook, sensing what's underneath the surface. You begin to see each day as a canvas for communion.

To stay in dialogue with reality, develop habits that keep you connected. You might begin each day by asking, "What do I need to see today?" or "Show me what matters most." Then go about your day with openness. Watch what themes emerge. Notice what grabs your attention and what fades. Listen to your body when it contracts or expands. Follow your curiosity without demanding an endpoint.

Journaling helps to capture the conversation. Write down your dreams, symbols, patterns, feelings. Not everything will make sense at once, but over time, you'll see threads emerge. You'll recognize how the Universe speaks to you, uniquely. You'll learn your symbolic language, your intuitive rhythms.

Also, practice speaking back. Not just through words, but through intention and action. If you receive a message—act on it. If you feel a nudge—follow it. The Universe doesn't just send signs as information. It sends them as invitations. Responding to them completes the loop. It turns awareness into embodiment.

And when things go quiet—because they will—don't assume you've lost the signal. Sometimes silence is a message, too. It may mean rest, trust, or integration. It may mean you're already aligned, and the next step is simply to live rather than interpret.

In this daily dialogue, you begin to feel less like a seeker and more like a participant. You're not waiting for the Universe to prove something. You're walking with it, co-authoring meaning in real time.

The 7-Day Sign Spotting Experiment

To truly integrate this practice into your life, try a 7-day experiment. Think of it as a tuning exercise—not to test the Universe, but to sharpen your attention and expand your capacity for presence. For one week, commit to tracking signs—not just obvious ones, but subtle signals, emotional impressions, and repeating themes. Here's how:

Day 1: Set the Tone
Begin with intention. Declare: "I am open to receiving guidance in all forms." Stay alert, but not anxious. At the end of the day, write down anything that felt significant—no matter how small.

Day 2: Tune Into Emotion
Pay special attention to how situations and people feel. What lights you up? What drains you? What excites or unsettles you? Emotions are the tuning forks of truth. Let them guide your awareness.

Day 3: Look for Repetition
Notice what repeats. This might be numbers, phrases, animals, ideas, or even song lyrics. Repetition is the Universe knocking louder. Ask: "What's this trying to tell me?"

Day 4: Practice Asking
Ask a question in the morning—something specific, heartfelt, and open-ended. Invite a sign in response. Then release attachment and go about your day. See what shows up.

Day 5: Reflect on Dreams
Keep a notepad or phone by your bed. When you wake up, jot down anything you remember. Even fragments. Dreams are your subconscious channeling Source without the interference of ego.

Day 6: Embody the Message
Choose one sign you've noticed and act on it. This could mean having a conversation, making a change, or simply resting. The point is to respond—to turn insight into alignment.

Day 7: Synthesize and Trust
Look back over your notes. What themes emerged? What surprised you? What became clearer? Celebrate what you received, and affirm: "This conversation never ends. I trust it will continue."

This practice is not just about collecting evidence. It's about strengthening your bond with something vast, wise, and subtle. It's about building a life where the mystical is not a separate realm—it's the water you swim in every day.

The End

Your reality is not silent. It's singing in symbols, nudging you in feelings, whispering in dreams, speaking through people, timing, resistance, ease. Every part of your life is part of the message. The more you open to this truth, the more miraculous your ordinary days become.

This isn't about chasing magic. It's about discovering that you are the magic—an active participant in a Universe that responds to your awareness with precision and grace.

The journey doesn't end here. In fact, this is where it begins: a life of listening, of acting in alignment, of co-creating with mystery. You no longer need to beg for signs. You no longer need to prove anything. You know now how to receive, how to trust, how to respond. You've learned to see, and seeing changes everything.

Let this awareness live not just in your thoughts, but in your walk, your breath, your decisions. Let your life become the clearest message of all—that you are here, awake, and willing to live the great unfolding with your eyes open.

Because the Universe is speaking.

And now, so are you.

www.ingramcontent.com/pod-product-compliance
Lightning Source LLC
Chambersburg PA
CBHW070930270326
41927CB00011B/2796